South-West England

South-West England

3500BC — AD600

Aileen Fox

David & Charles : Newton Abbot

o 7153 6209 7

First published by Thames & Hudson in 1964
Revised edition published by David & Charles in 1973
© Aileen Fox 1964, 1973

Set in 11 on 13 pt Imprint
and printed in Great Britain
by Ebenezer Baylis & Son Ltd
The Trinity Press Worcester and London
for David & Charles (Holdings) Limited
South Devon House Newton Abbot Devon

Contents

List of Illustrations

PLATES

7

FIGURES

Preface to the First Edition

I have long wanted to write a book about the archaeology of south-west England, in which it would be possible to consider the early human settlement of the peninsula as a whole and to forget about county boundaries. I am deeply grateful to the Editor, Dr Glyn Daniel, for suggesting that it should be included in this series and for waiting until I was free to write it. I am conscious now of its imperfections, realising that with the increasing flow of new discoveries, excavations and the re-assessment of old material, it is almost impossible to get everything correctly focused in the short compass of this volume. I have been enabled to make this attempt by the kindness of many friends and fellow-workers who have discussed the various problems and who have given me information in advance of publication: I am particularly indebted in this way to Arthur ApSimon, Professor J. D. Evans, Peter Fowler, C. A. Ralegh Radford, Andrew Saunders, Charles Thomas, Bernard Wailes and Dr F. S. Wallis. In addition I have benefited from the informed criticism of Leo Rivet in Chapters VII and VIII and from advice from C. E. Stevens in Chapter IX.

For assistance with the illustrations I am much indebted to my former students Gillian Lamacraft (Mrs Mitchell) and Christine Wilkins, as well as Mr R. Fry and Miss R. Bethell, technicians in the Department of Geography and Mr W. Hoskin, the University photographer. I should also like to acknowledge with gratitude the helpful co-operation of the curators of the museums at Exeter, Taunton and Truro in placing objects at our disposal for photography, and also the kindness of Mr

Charles Wolfe of Newquay in allowing me to select photographs of sites from his collection. The final form of the maps I owe to the skill of Mr H. A. Shelley.

28 St Leonard's Road   A.F.
 Exeter
December 1963

Preface to the Revised Edition

Almost ten years have elapsed since I wrote the text of *South-West England* and during that time much archaeological research has taken place in the area, as in Britain generally. Ideas about the nature of the past have changed: thanks to radio-carbon dating and the recent advances in dendrochronology of the bristle-cone pine, we know that man's past in the British Isles as in Europe is far longer than previously supposed. We lay more stress on the continuity of population, and no longer interpret every change of pottery style as implying a folk movement to these islands. I have tried in this second edition to take account of this change of emphasis, as well as describing new discoveries and excavations and bringing the nomenclature into line with present use. All the distribution maps have been brought up to date, three new ones added, as well as plans of sites and photographs of several outstanding objects. I am only too well aware there can be no finality and that much of what I have now written will need to be rewritten in another decade. Some fundamentals remain: Chapter I is virtually unchanged.

Although this book is no longer part of Thames and Hudson's Ancient Peoples and Places series, the approach is the same. This is not a handbook to the archaeology of Devon and Cornwall—though it may be used as such sometimes for the lack of anything else—but an account of the prehistoric and early historic peoples in the south-west peninsula as seen by one working archaeologist. In attempting to cover such a wide field it is obvious that I have had to rely on the work of others, as shown in the enlarged bibliography at the end of the book. Some omissions are deliberate, such as the Palaeolithic period and, regretfully, the intermittent references to the Scilly Isles: these are a reflection of the writer's limitations of interest in time, space and seamanship. As before I am much indebted to friends and colleagues for criticisms, suggestions and information: in particular to Dr Isobel Smith and Frances Lynch (Mrs Llewellyn) for problems of the Neolithic in Chapters II–III; to Miss Susan Pearce (Mrs Macmillan) for Bronze Age metal-work in Chapters V–VI; to Michael Griffiths for information about new discoveries in Exeter, which together with my own work with Professor W. Ravenhill, has meant that much of Chapter VIII has been rewritten; and to Anne Hamlin and Susan Pearce for Chapter IX. Not all of the suggestions have been adopted, because this remains a personal book.

2 The Retreat
Topsham   AILEEN FOX
December 1972

CHAPTER I

The Place

CHARACTER AND RELIEF
The sea is never far away in the south-west; even on the high moorlands, on Dartmoor and Bodmin, there is a gleam on the horizon and nearing the Atlantic coast the windswept land flattens, the colours in the landscape brighten and the character of the peninsula asserts itself. Lying with its long axis east and west, it extends on the north from Bridgewater Bay and on the south from Lyme Regis Bay to the granite cliffs of Land's End, a distance of approximately 130 miles: at its widest, from Prawle Point, Salcombe to the Foreland at Lynton, it is about 75 miles across, narrowing to some 20 miles from Padstow to St Austell westwards. The western coast faces the Atlantic which pounds at a line of sheer cliffs from Land's End to Morte Point, the northern fronts the Bristol Channel looking across to South Wales, whilst the south coast, which is more indented, is at the end of the English Channel as it widens to meet the ocean. Ringed by salt water in this way, the peninsula has received sea-borne immigrants from varied sources in prehistoric times and its inhabitants have established a wide range of overseas trading contacts, particularly with the continental Atlantic coasts.

Geographically it is somewhat set apart from the rest of England, not only by the surrounding seas but by a large area of fen and marsh, the Somerset Levels, which extend from the foot of the Mendip hills to the Quantocks and for over 20 miles inland. Consequently there is a tendency for individual cultures to develop in the region which differ from the southern norm.

It is not a mountainous country: the relief presents no barrier to its penetration as the Welsh hills do. The greater part of the land ranges from between 200 to 600 feet; only on Exmoor, Dartmoor and Bodmin Moor are there extensive areas above 1,000ft, and these are rolling grass and heather moorlands capable of supporting a considerable prehistoric population under favourable climatic conditions. Although on a small scale, the relief is readily distinguishable and forms the key to an understanding of the region. Early man, lacking maps, would soon have learnt to recognise the pattern of the hills and rivers. The 400–800ft Land's End peninsula dominates the horizon of west Cornwall, as does Bodmin Moor, rising to 1,375ft, in east Cornwall. The mass of Dartmoor, with its summits of High Willhayes (2,039ft) in the north and Ryder's Hill (1,692ft) on the south is conspicuous on the skyline over the greater part of Devon, whilst the long west-to-east line of Exmoor (highest on Dun-

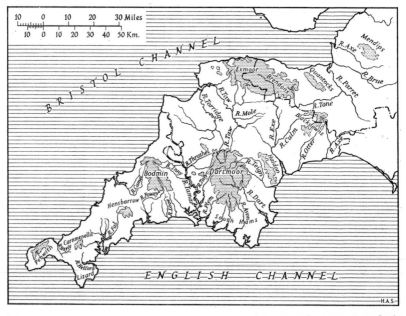

Fig 1 Relief map of the south-west. Land over 1,000ft is stippled ; county boundaries are shown by a broken line

kery Beacon 1,706ft) with an extension in the Brendon Hills (1,340ft) forms a landmark to the north. In the east the northern escarpment of the Blackdowns (800ft) is also conspicuous, as well as the Quantock and Mendip ridges flanking the Somerset marsh. The principal rivers, the Exe, Teign, Dart, Plym, Tamar, Fowey and Fal, flow to the south coast: only the Taw and Torridge in mid-Devon, the Camel in Corn-wall, and the Axe, Brue and Parrett in Somerset drain to the Bristol Channel. Consequently the south coast provides a succession of deep estuaries and natural harbours with a hinterland that is much dissected by steep-sided wooded valleys, whilst on the north there is an extensive coastal plateau, unbroken from the Camel to Hartland Point, lacking any sheltered anchorage.

GEOLOGICAL STRUCTURE

In the main it is an ancient land, composed of Palaeozoic and igneous rocks heavily worn down and eroded, with a succession of later forma-tions overlying them in south-east Devon, and Somerset.

The earliest rocks make up the bold southerly promontories of the Lizard, Dodman and Bolt Head with Start Point. The remainder of the peninsula consists of the Devonian formations of sedimentary rocks, hard grits, sandstones, slates, limestones, and shales, which have been squeezed by north-south pressures into east-west folds in the Armorican earth movements at the close of the Carboniferous era. Exmoor and the Quantocks form the present summit of one such major fold; they dip southward into a great trough or syncline in mid-Devon in which the Carboniferous Culm Measures lie, and then rise again to reappear in south Devon and Cornwall. Pushed up into, and now appearing above them, are the five granite masses, Dartmoor, Bodmin Moor, Hens-barrow (St Austell), Carnmenellis, and Penwith, each surrounded by rocks altered by contact with the molten mass and known as the meta-morphic aureole. Igneous rocks also intruded into the fissures that de-veloped in the sedimentaries around the granite upheavals and gave rise to dykes, mainly of elvan, which show now as slender ridges or bands of hard outcrop, some extending for several miles in Cornwall.

B 17

Overlying the eastern edge of the Culm are the New Red sandstones, the Permian and Triassic sands, marls and breccias, with a warm red colour which typifies the arid desert conditions at the time they were laid down. These extend from Torbay northwards and eastwards, and are conspicuous in the fields in the lower Exe and Culm valleys and in the eroded cliffs of the south coast as far as Sidmouth. Triassic marls also occur extensively in the Vale of Taunton. The succeeding Jurassic formations are marine deposits of Lias clay and limestones present in Somerset.

Finally, the Cretaceous formations are represented only in east Devon by a small coastal strip of chalk, best seen in the 300ft cliff of Beer Head, with its seams of flint so important to early man, and by Greensand which forms a dissected plateau extending from the coast between Sidmouth and Lyme Regis and rising inland to form the Blackdown Hills. The Haldon ridge is a greensand outlier between the Exe and Teign valleys, which has a capping of chert and flinty gravel.

The low-lying area of the Somerset Levels is a trough eroded out of the soft Mesozoic sediments, which was filled after a marine transgression at the end of the glaciations by alluvial clays, and then by a succession of peats which were formed when the inland waters were ponded back by the estuarine muds and sand dunes of Bridgewater Bay. This peat growth continued, with fluctuations, during prehistoric and early historic times. The district thus became a fenland traversed by the narrow Lias ridge of the Polden Hills which divides the Brue and the Parrett.

SOILS

This outline of the geology indicates the variety of terrain that makes up the south-west and the different soils it contains. The Devonian sandstones produce a shallow, acid soil as on Exmoor, usually very stony, whilst the slates and killas in south Devon and Cornwall break down into a 'shillet', that is, slivers of rock. The granite breaks up into a coarse gritty sand, orange or yellow in colour, known as 'rab' in Cornwall or 'growan' in Devon. The patches of Devonian limestone in the hinterland of Torbay and at Plymouth produce a shallow calcareous soil. All these pervious soils over the Palaeozoic rocks have one thing in common; they nourish a woodland that is dry underfoot and free of undergrowth, which when it is cleared, produces good open grazing.

In contrast, the Culm Measures break down into a stiff yellow clay, water-logged in winter, hard-baked in summer, and supporting a dense mixed oakwood with a heavy undergrowth which rendered the greater part of mid-Devon unfit for early settlement. Nevertheless there are tracts where the bands of Culm sandstone or shale are exposed or near the surface, as in the Halwill district, north-west of Okehampton or in the Atlantic coastal tract between Stratton and Hartland; the soil here is lighter and better drained and consequently under favourable climatic conditions, as in the Bronze Age, these areas were occupied. The red soils of the Permian are deep, friable and fertile marls; they carry much woodland and therefore were not extensively settled till Saxon times. The Greensands produce acid sandy soils, often full of broken chert but suitable for early settlement.

CLIMATE

The rainfall in the south-west, as is well known, is double that of south-east England; in Devon it averages today about 40in whilst on Dartmoor this rises to 80in or more in places. This is due to factors that are constant. The prevailing winds are westerly, warmed by their long passage across the Atlantic: rain-laden clouds impinge here first of all and discharge, or they descend in sea mists along the coasts or in hill-fogs on the moors. Great gales engendered in Biscay or far out on the Atlantic drive furiously across the peninsula, whipping up the seas and tearing at the trees. Consequently there are two contrary climatic factors affecting the western landscape: in sheltered places well-watered vegetation grows lush in the warm and humid air, and even in winter the grass is green; but in exposed places, the trees are shorn and stunted by the winds and the moorlands have only a grass and heather covering which is bleak and austere. This in turn had consequences for early peoples in the region. Settlers looked for shelter from rain and wind for their huts, not in the

deep valleys filled with luxuriant tree growth, but in those on the upland (Plate 12b). Hill-forts were built not only on the crests, but on the
hill-slopes, or tucked away down at the sheltered end of a spur, despite
the loss of defensive advantage and outlook. Economically, the wet
climate could be made an asset because it enabled herds of cattle to be
built up to take advantage of the abundant grass and water supplies. On
the other hand the uncertainties of large-scale corn-growing were
avoided in a land where the stony ground was hard to till and the damp
grain difficult to harvest and to store.

NATURAL RESOURCES

The varied geological structure provided early man with stones for
building, for implements and ornaments and, above all, with metal ores.

Building stones confronted settlers practically everywhere; huts and
enclosures (Plates 12, 23) were made of local material, particularly of
the granite clitter on Bodmin Moor, Dartmoor and Land's End. In so
doing, people helped themselves by clearing the land of stones, im-
proving the grazing or making some tillage possible. For the same
reason most of the burial mounds in the region are cairns (that is, stone
heaps) which were piled over a stone chamber or box-like cist.

This widespread use of stone is an advantage; stone structures survive, whilst wood and clay, the building materials of most of southern
Britain, leave no surface trace. Since there has been little urban or industrial development in the region, a high proportion of monuments
remain today in a setting that has not changed radically from prehistoric
times. In districts like Dartmoor (Plate 6b) or West Penwith, groups of
religious and funeral monuments and numerous early settlements are
preserved which give even the casual visitor a picture of early man in
relation to his environment. For the archaeologist this wealth of material
is a great asset; it is possible, for instance, to assess the number of
households making up a community, to ascertain the acreage cultivated
by a single family, or with the aid of excavation to ascertain their economy (Fig 29).

On the other hand, the archaeologist is handicapped by the destructive character of the acid soils in most of the region. These dissolve human and animal bones, corrode bronzes to green powder and iron to shapeless lumps, and they soften the hand-made Bronze Age pottery, usually badly-fired and of poor clay in the first place, so that it disintegrates. Consequently finds from an excavation frequently are few and may give a misleading impression of poverty. Only in the bogs when the oxygen is excluded by the peat cover, or in the sands, do things survive well; at the Somerset lake villages of Meare and Glastonbury the decoration on wooden tubs is preserved and bronzes still retain their golden colour.

METALS

The real riches of the south-west are its mineral ores: of these, gold, tin, copper, lead with its associated silver and some iron were utilised in prehistoric and Roman times. Metal-bearing lodes in Devon and Cornwall are intimately related to the granite, since they are the products of vapours and solutions filling the fissures which developed as the molten rock mass cooled and solidified (Fig 2). Prolonged erosion through millennia exposed the surface of the veins and weathered them: swollen streams brought down pebbles of cassiterite from the tin lodes and deposited them along with granite debris in the gravels of the river beds. In prehistoric times, the full potential of the region was never realised, since the lodes slope steeply downwards at 30°–45°, and the greater part lies too deep to be reached until the development of modern mining machinery. Early man was dependent on finding outcrops that could be worked open-cast or by shallow adits, and in the case of tin and rare gold, by digging in alluvial gravels. The veins of ore would attract attention in the first place by the reddening of the surrounding rock, as can still be seen in the cliffs at St Just. The dark tinstone (cassiterite) or the yellow glint of copper sulphide (calcopyrite) would also be conspicuous by the associated bands of white quartz, and their characteristic close texture and heavy weight would also have served as a guide.

The richness of the south-west in tin is well known but it is less generally appreciated that copper, the other component of bronze, is also present, admittedly now at depth. Both minerals are found together in Cornwall, principally in the Land's End peninsula, in the Camborne–Redruth district, and south-east of Bodmin Moor (Fig 2). On Dartmoor stream tin is widely distributed in the river valleys and copper occurs in the metamorphic aureole, principally in the Dart valley above Buckfast and around Tavistock and Gunnislake. This distribution ensured that most of the best mining areas were accessible from the south coast, where as we have seen, there are good harbours and deep estuaries.

Silver and lead ores occur sporadically in Cornwall, in the Callington district as argentiferous copper, and at Combe Martin in north Devon; but until the introduction of a coinage at the end of the Iron Age, and the fashion for fine tableware in Roman times, silver was not in demand. The principal source was then the Mendip hills in Somerset, where there are extensive remains of Roman mining.

Iron ores too are present in the south-west and there is evidence that they were utilised in the later prehistoric period. Limonite could be recognised by its rusty colour or slaggy appearance and haematite by the red streak that a piece will give if rubbed on any flat surface, as well as by the weight. The lodes are associated with the granite, but being in the mineral group that crystallised at lower temperatures than tin or copper, they are found, for the most part, farther away. The deposits of specular haematite associated with the Dartmoor granite occur in the lower Teign valley, and in Cornwall in the St Agnes district. Iron oxides are also found in the overburden of the tin and copper lodes forming the deposit known as gossan or 'iron hat'. Small quantities of limonite occur as bog-iron concretions.

Mineral ores, then, are abundant, accessible and fairly widespread in the region. Man had to learn to recognise them as the source of the different metals he successively required and to discover different ways to transmute the stony ores into tactile substances. The archaeological evidence for how this was achieved is not straightforward. There is nothing comparable with the late Bronze Age copper mines in the Austrian Tyrol, for example, where the adits, tip-heaps and smelting places remain on the Schiefer Alp. In our region traces of shallow prehistoric or Roman workings have been obliterated by the systematic exploitation of historic times, and only scanty remains of smelting hearths and small furnaces have occasionally been found in settlements (Fig 31). Fortunately there is the well-known account of tin working by the Greek historian Diodorus Siculus (v: 22) writing in the first century BC; he narrates how the metal was dug from earthy veins in the rock, ground down and smelted into ingots shaped like knuckle-bones *(astragali)*, and then carried across the sands in waggons to the island of St Michael's Mount *(Ictis)* at low tide. From here it was shipped by Gallic traders to western ports in Gaul and then by an overland route to the Mediterranean at the mouth of the Rhône. For the rest, the periods at which the metal was worked have to be inferred from the discovery of dateable objects in the mining areas. Occasionally an exotic find from overseas or from other parts of Britain reveals the source from which traders came to buy. Irish merchants can thus be detected in Cornwall in the early Bronze Age bringing gold *lunulae* (Plate 8b) or Dobunnic

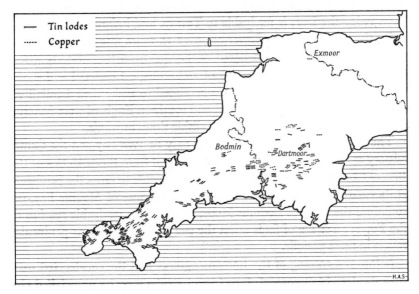

Fig 2 Distribution of tin and copper lodes

merchants from the Cotswolds exchanging iron currency bars for the local tin at Holne on the Dart. The south-west was not Eldorado; it did not grow rich on its metals. Even in the Iron Age when the tin trade was most flourishing, the Cornish chieftains and their ladies had relatively few fine possessions and for the mass of the people, the pastoral mode of life was little changed. In Roman times, precious metals were a state monopoly and therefore of little material benefit to the locality.

COMMUNICATIONS

For traders and invaders coming to the south-west, seaways were of more importance than landways. The southern flank of the peninsula has a series of inviting entries by the dozen rivers from the Axe to the Fal (Fig 1). Many of these are 'rias', drowned river valleys formed when the sea levels rose in post-glacial times. Their deep water channels could carry shallow-draught vessels far inland, through the steep-sided lower reaches where the green canopy of the woods in summer comes down to the water, towards the moorland hills which beckoned on the horizon. Even today the Dart is navigable to Totnes, and before the weirs were built, the tides ran up to Staverton, over 12 miles from the coast. The estuaries also provide a sheltered anchorage from the westerly gales. Consequently, as the distribution of archaeological material will show, peoples coming from western Europe aimed to make their landfall on this coast and contacts with Dorset and southern England were fostered by the ease of coastal traffic from Neolithic times onwards.

The stormy north Cornish coast has only St Ives Bay and the Camel estuary at Padstow for voyagers approaching it from the Irish Sea or the Bristol Channel. From these ports it was possible to cross the peninsula at its narrowest points, either to the sandy expanse of Mounts Bay, or, rounding the flank of Bodmin Moor, to reach the navigable reaches of the Fowey: a string of finds attest the use of these two trans-peninsular routes in most periods.

Before the coming of the Roman engineer and the constructed road with its straight alignment, travel was by ridgeway, by unmetalled circuitous tracks which by sticking closely to the watersheds avoid descents

1a, b (*left*)
Early Neolithic
pottery bowls
from Hembury,
East Devon.
Height 6·8in.
and 4·8in.
Exeter
Museum
1c (*right*)
Stone axe,
Group I, in
birch wood
haft from
Port Talbot,
Glamorgan.
Axe length
6·7in.
National
Museum of
Wales

2 (above) Carn Gluze, St Just, West Cornwall: the central area, with the primary pit and domed cairn
3a (below) Chamber tomb at Pawton, Wadebridge, Cornwall

3b (*below*) Zennor Quoit chamber tomb, Zennor, West Cornwall

4a *(above)* Idol of ash wood, from beneath the Bell track, Westhay, Somerset. Height 155mm, 6·2in. Cambridge Museum of Archaeology and Ethnology 4b *(below left)* The Abbot's way, Neolithic track, near Westhay, Somerset 4c *(below right)* Reconstruction of the Neolithic long bow of yew wood from Meare Heath, Somerset. Cambridge Museum of Archaeology and Ethnology

into the wooded valleys and the crossing of streams. The complicated structure of Devon and Cornwall, where the pattern of the relief is interrupted by the granite masses, does not lend itself to a long-distance east-west route comparable with the Icknield Way or the Berkshire ridgeway. Instead there are a number of short north-south routes related to the hill systems, such as those on the Greensand in east Devon, or in the South Hams, or in the Looe–Fowey district in south Cornwall. Their use is attested by the distribution of barrows, hill-forts and chance finds.

On the rolling moorlands above the tree line there was greater freedom of movement. The small streams on Bodmin and Dartmoor are not difficult to cross in the upper valleys, and the bogs that are now obstacles have developed mainly since the climatic deterioration early in the Iron Age, so traffic was not canalised. In north Devon there is a ridgeway sign-posted by barrow groups from the coast at Morte Bay to Blackmoor Gate, and another going south-east on the high ground from Challacombe Common, on the line of the present county boundary. In west Somerset the sparsely populated Brendon Hills are linked with Exmoor and with the Blackdowns by an east–west ridgeway and the Quantocks have a north–south route leading to a crossing of the Tone at Taunton.

The difficulties of crossing the Somerset levels have already been mentioned; both in the Neolithic period and in the late Bronze Age, when the climate rapidly deteriorated, timber tracks were laid in the valley of the Brue and on Shapwick Heath for crossing the low ground to the Polden ridge along which NW–SE traffic was always possible, 150 feet above the marshes. In sum, in the south-western peninsula, land-travel by ridgeway or across open moor was possible for relatively short distances in the areas suitable for occupation; long-distance travel was by sea.

CHAPTER II

The Neolithic Peoples

It is always difficult to decide at what point to launch into the stream of human history. The concern of the archaeologist in a region is with change and succession, with peoples' coming and going, the establishment of their economy, with the development of tools and weapons, the variations in pottery-making, house or tomb building, and with the expansion or contraction of settlement areas: there are no fixed points at which to begin or end in the flow of time.

The arbitrary point selected in this book is the arrival in the south-west of a people from western France with a Neolithic culture, according to radio-carbon dating between 3500 and 3000 BC. The arrival may well be six or seven hundred years earlier according to calculations based on the recent tree-ring analysis of the bristle cone pine. The new-comers were communities who had already mastered the arts of pottery making and of specialised flint working and who had knowledge of the raising and management of cattle and sheep, and of the cultivation of grain. The mixed economy of the West Country farmer was theirs in embryo and they were tied to the soil, the seasons and their pastures as is their modern counterpart. In this they differed fundamentally from the earlier Mesolithic groups who were semi-nomadic, living by hunting, fishing and collecting of their food supplies.

At this time the country was much as we have described it in Chapter I; with the exception of the high moorlands, a mixed oak forest had grown extensively in the warm wet Atlantic climate that had set in about 5000 BC, succeeding the cold dry Boreal phase in which pine and birch forests predominated. Pollen analysis on Dartmoor by I. A. Simmons has shown that the blanket peat bog began to form in the Neolithic period and that oak and alder formed the highest proportion of the wind-borne tree pollens at its base, followed by wych-elm, birch and also a little lime indicating that the upland was wooded. Similarly in the Somerset levels a marine transgression *c* 4000 BC succeeded by freshwater swamps was a result of the same climatic amelioration; these were followed by the growth of alder and birch woods which in turn were swamped by the development of raised bogs with sphagnum before 2000 BC.

The newcomers were experienced in forest clearance and had developed a characteristic tool, the stone axe mounted on a wooden haft (Plate 1c), the endurance and efficiency of which was increased by polishing the axe head. With its aid for felling and by bark-ringing and burning, cultivation patches could be cut out of the forests; and the grazing of the livestock then kept the ground clear. A gradual amelioration of the climate in the second millennium BC, the Sub-Boreal phase, also helped to check regeneration of the woods.

The people who formed the basis of the primary Neolithic population in the south-west are known as yet only from their settlements and from chance finds of their possessions. Their physical appearance, however, can be established from the skeletons of their contemporaries inhumed under long barrows in southern England. They were of small stature, lightly boned and neatly built, with delicately fashioned hands and feet, indicating good powers of movement and skill; they had long thin faces, and probably a swarthy complexion, not unlike the North American Indian. They arrived in southern England over a long period of time in the fourth and early third millennia BC, bringing with them into the empty wooded lands their seed-corn, their stock and their skills in craft. The boats in which they travelled are not known but we may suppose it was in some sort of a skin-boat like the Irish curraghs which are seaworthy in the Atlantic swells.

In our area, the indigenous Mesolithic inhabitants were few and confined to the coasts and open moors. Their hearths and chipping floors at which microliths (tiny flint blades with blunt backs) were produced, have been found on the cliffs in Penwith, on the north Cornish and Devon coasts and also around Dozemary Pool on Bodmin Moor. Little groups occur around spring heads, as at Week, Dartmoor, and on sand hills, as at Gwithian. They lived a semi-nomadic existence, depending for their food supply on fish, birds, deer and other wild creatures which abounded in the woods and streams and on shellfish from the coasts.

SETTLEMENTS

The distinctive group of Neolithic people who settled in south-west England were probably among the earliest to arrive in southern Britain

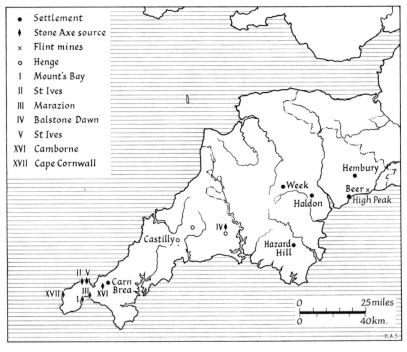

Fig 3 Distribution of Neolithic settlements and centres of stone axe production

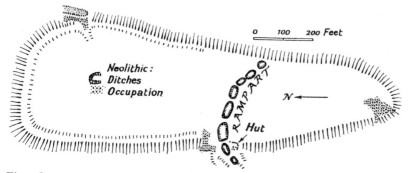

Fig 4 Causewayed camp at Hembury, Devon. The hachures mark the inner rampart of the Iron Age fort

from the continent. Their hill-top settlements range from Carn Brea near Camborne to Maiden Castle in Dorset, (Fig 3). The most important is the causewayed camp at Hembury, east Devon, which first produced the pottery that differentiates these south-western communities from the related Windmill Hill peoples of Wiltshire and Sussex, and which radiocarbon analysis has now shown to have been occupied from about 3320–3000 BC.

Hembury is on the tip of a steep-sided spur of greensand at the end of the Blackdown Hills, north-west of Honiton and about 12 miles from the coast. The site has obvious defensive advantages and consequently was strongly fortified by the Celtic people in the Iron Age (Plate 16d) and it was during the systematic excavation of the hill-fort by the late Dorothy Liddell in 1930–35 that the Neolithic settlement came to light (Fig 4). The end of the spur was enclosed by eight lengths of ditches aligned as a segment of a circle across the ridge and the soil heaped up as a bank on their south side. The ditches were of a characteristic U-shaped profile, and were separated by causeways of varying width which may have been left for no other reason than that sufficient soil had been obtained for the bank. There was an entrance at the west end, where there was a setting of five posts in two rows across a causeway, a framework for some sort of gate or a barricade: immediately inside was a timber hut. The settlement, however, was not confined within the

crescent of ditches and bank, but extended northwards to another ditch
with an external palisade on the east side of the hill. Whether this was
part of a second line of interrupted ditches crossing the spur could not
be ascertained, owing to the overlying Iron Age defences, but it seems
likely that Hembury consisted of two or more enclosures, like the
majority of its kind. It thus represents the adaption of the concentric
plan, familiar from Windmill Hill or the Trundle, to a promontory site.
At Hambledon, Dorset, the outer zone of a Neolithic settlement was
defined similarly by short lines of ditches across the spurs.

The Neolithic people lived in the lee of their ramparts and on the tip
of the spur. Beneath the Iron Age deposits and covered by a band of
sterile soil representing the vegetation that had grown over the hill after
their settlement was abandoned, there was a thick layer of burning and
occupation debris with stone-edged hearths and small shallow pits.
Some of the pits had been used for food storage, as was shown by car-
bonised grain and hazel nuts; in one there was a complete bag-shaped
pot (Plate 1a) so placed to keep liquid, such as curdled milk for cheese,
safe from upset and at an even temperature. Other pits were probably
ovens used for roasting meat or fish amongst heated stones and ashes.
In time they ceased to be used and gradually filled up with rubbish, as
is shown by Miss Liddell's discovery of a place 'where a pot of wheat
had been upset, the grain lying thick upon the edge of the pit and spray-
ing out over the slope'. With it was a large piece of pottery with grains
adhering to its inner surface. The dwellings associated with all this
activity were ill-defined, no more than a curved setting of stones and an
occasional post-hole; they must have been lightly-built, with walls of
wattle-work daubed over with clay on the stone base, and thatched with
heather or reeds. Only the oval or sub-rectangular hut by the entrance—
the so-called guard-house—had a substantial frame of seventeen close-
set posts. Occupation-rubbish was deposited in the ditches and burnt
there and then covered by soil pushed down from the bank. Above the
primary silt in most sectors there was a pronounced layer of burning in
one place nearly 2ft deep, which had reddened the side of the ditch for
3ft up the slope. Charcoal from this layer gave a radiocarbon date of

3330 BC ± 150, which can be compared with 3240 BC ± 150 from charcoals from the occupation area, and 3300–3000 BC from a sample from the bottom of the ditch.

From the extent, density, and character of the occupation, Hembury appears to have been a settlement inhabited for some 300–500 years. The frequency of grain in the pits, which a recent examination has shown to be emmer, a small wheat *(Triticum dicoccum)* naked and hulled barley *(Hordeum)* and possibly also some spelt *(Triticum spelta)* and of the saucer-shaped saddle querns for grinding, indicates that the occupants were arable farmers. The picture of their economy is necessarily incomplete because no animal bones survived in the acid soil; only the ubiquitous flint scrapers, of which 600 were found, attests to the preparation of skins for leather clothing, thongs, bags, etc, and shows that they were also stock breeders.

Hembury, then, is a contrast with other causewayed camps in southern England like Windmill Hill, which apparently were places used only seasonally for social and religious gatherings, though over a long period of time. A brief glance at the other hill-top settlements in the region (Fig 3) shows that they are akin to Hembury. At Hazard Hill (400ft) above the Harbourne river west of Totnes, a prolific flint industry was associated with pottery in small pits, hearths and cooking holes and with occasional post-holes dug in the shillet; saucer querns were also present, implying cultivation. The larger storage pits were probably lined with wickerwork and their capacity of 14 to 17 cubic feet was sufficient to hold 13 to 15 bushels of grain, enough to feed a family of four for a year. Smaller pits were probably for storing water in a skin bag or for standing pots as at Hembury. All eventually became filled with rubbish. At Haldon, on the top of the 800ft ridge dividing the Exe and Teign and accessible by eight miles of ridgeway from the coast, the remains of a sizeable rectangular house were found (Fig 5). It had a frame of timber uprights 2 to 4 feet apart and a gabled roof carried on a ridge-pole indicated by two post-holes on the central axis. The daub walls rested on a rough foundation of small stones set in clay, with a doorway in the north-east corner and there was a stone-edged hearth

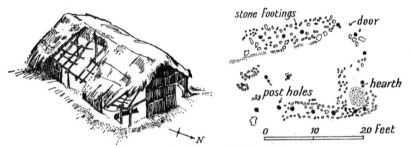

Fig 5 Reconstruction of a Neolithic house at Haldon, Devon

in the south-east angle. The clay floor was trodden hard and had been raised and renewed: a thick deposit of ash against the north wall and partly underlying it, also indicated a long occupation. Like Hazard, the settlement was apparently open; the impression of a grain of wheat on a potsherd indicates that corn was grown here also.

At Carn Brea near Redruth, Cornwall, the settlement was on the south-east flank of the 700ft hill, which was fortified later by the Iron Age people. Characteristic western Neolithic pottery was found here below the floors of huts belonging to the hill-fort when these were excavated in the nineteenth century, as well as several stone axes and many leaf-shaped flint arrowheads. Recent excavation has identified a group of two or three small dry-stone huts situated on a terrace below an outcrop and enclosed by a low stone wall. Some of the level ground on the hill top had been cleared of loose granite presumably for cultivation at this time.

High Peak is a heavily eroded cliff-top 500ft high, west of Sidmouth, which was fortified in the post-Roman period (p. 193) but also occupied in early Neolithic times, within the period 3130–2830 BC. A typical flat-bottomed ditch delimited the eastern side of the Neolithic settlement. No houses were identified but there were signs that the underlying chert had been quarried for building. There were many hearths and shallow pits, including two that had been carefully lined with flints for storage. There are probably many more hill-top settlements awaiting discovery in the south-west; most of those described were invisible on the surface and only found during the excavation of the conspicuous later fortifications.

POTTERY

The domestic pottery produced by these people is nearly all plain ware, wide-mouthed bowls and baggy pots with unsteady rounded bases and simple flat or pinched-out rims: many have lugs to lift them with, either solid little bosses or perforated vertically for a thong (Plate 1a). These basic shapes are common to a wide range of early Neolithic peoples both in Britain and in western Europe, as at the first lake settlement at Cortaillod, Switzerland. Of special importance because they are peculiar to the south-west are bowls with big incurved lugs, perforated horizontally and christened 'trumpet lugs' from their expanded ends (Plate 1b): analogies for these are found in the earlier wares from the Camp de Chassey in the Massif Central and in a few megalithic tombs in Brittany, Castellic and Kervilor. A few bowls from Hembury and some others coming principally from Carn Brea have a carination break below a straight neck, a specialised western form which appears in settlements at Clegyr Boia, Pembrokeshire and at Lough Gur in Co Cork.

A flat-based pot from Haldon decorated with two zones of incised vertical lines stands rather apart from this series, although it was associated with it on the site. It may be a later product of the group comparable with Rinyo-Clacton grooved wares in the south and east.

Though the shapes are unsophisticated, Neolithic fabrics are surprisingly good, finer than much Bronze Age pottery. Most of it is a dark brownish ware, often with a smooth leathery surface, produced by the potter working over the finished pot with wet hands. The clays were tempered with coarse grits, usually of quartz or chert, obtainable in the locality. There is also a distinctive thin reddish ware with fine grits which petrological analysis by Dr David Peacock has shown were of gabbro, derived from the igneous rocks occurring only in the Lizard peninsula (Fig 6). The carinated bowls and those with trumpet lugs at Hembury are of this ware (f/ware) and it is also recorded in small quantities at all the south-western settlements. More surprising bowls of this

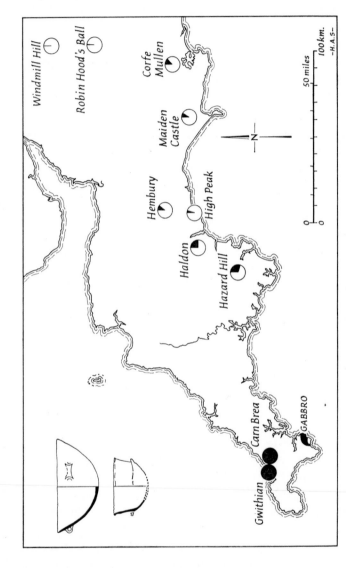

Fig 6 Source and distribution of Neolithic pottery of south-western origin; symbols show the proportion of gabbroic grits at each site

identical fabric have been found in the causewayed camps at Maiden Castle, Dorset, and at Robin Hood's Ball and Windmill Hill in Wiltshire. Such pots are unlikely to have been taken empty so far from their place of origin and whilst their perishable contents are unknown, salt is a possible trading commodity, needed for healthy livestock. Alternatively some merchant-venturers may have taken the bowls to hold their own seasonal food supplies and afterwards used them for barter or gifts.

FLINT-WORKING

The stone industry of these early Neolithic peoples indicates even more clearly than the pottery, their capacity to exploit the local resources and to organise long-distance travel (Fig 3). In Cornwall beach flint was used but in Devon the material for the numerous leaf-shaped arrowheads, scrapers and blades was the mottled blue or black unpatinated flint from the chalk at Beer Head. The mining places at Beer have not been located but there are many hollows and waste heaps just below the edge of the 400ft plateau, at a level which coincides with the bands of flint nodules exposed in the cliffs. Flint-working floors are frequent on the chalk plateau of the Head, an area of about $2\frac{1}{2}$ square miles; only small implements were made here, roughouts for axes being significantly absent. The amount of flint waste at Hembury, Haldon and Hazard Hill shows that it was the raw material that was sought at Beer, not finished products. Flint knapping was also in evidence at High Peak, where thirty implements and flakes were found in a tidy heap, placed originally perhaps in a skin bag.

The communities must have made regular visits by ridgeway or by sea, landing in the shelter east of Beer Head. Some flint axes were apparently imported ready-made from the chalk farther east: fifteen were found at Hembury of a grey flint and about twenty more have been recorded as surface finds from Cornwall and Devon. The distribution indicates sea traffic, with entries at Mounts Bay and Plymouth Sound.

THE AXE TRADE

This trade in axes was a two-way trade: the Neolithic peoples of the chalk were ready to purchase polished axes of the sombre igneous rocks, the greenstones of the south-west, which had blades less liable to fracture and were so different in appearance from the flint in general use (Plate 1c). The sources of stone axe production are now known from petrological analysis, undertaken from 1937 onwards by Dr F. S. Wallis and the late Dr J. F. S. Stone for a committee of the South-West Museums. By cutting a thin section from an axe and examining it microscopically it is possible to identify the constituents of the rock and to study their form and arrangement; on this basis a high proportion of the axes have been classified into 19 groups and closely related sub-groups. It has been possible to match exactly some of these sections with specimens of actual rocks and thus identify, within close limits, their places of manufacture both in Cornwall and elsewhere. This cannot always be done because the composition of the metamorphic rocks is highly variable and may change even in one exposure, and the variation may not be recorded in the available geological collections. However, greenstone axes of Groups II and V have been shown to emanate from St Ives, Group III from Trenow, Marazion, Group IV from Balstone Down, Callington, Group XVI from near Camborne, and XVII from Kenidjack Castle, in Penwith: in the case of the prolific Group I, the Mousehole–Penzance district is indicated but the actual outcrop is probably now submerged. Groups IA, IIA, IIIA, IVA, and XIX remain unmatched, although Cornwall is probably their most likely source.

Despite these indications from the petrologists, archaeologists have not yet discovered any of the Cornish quarries or factories. Elsewhere, at Graig Lwyd in Caernarvonshire and Great Langdale in Cumberland for instance, the sites have been located from the heaps of waste and incomplete or broken tools. It is evident from the number of south-western axes that cannot be grouped that small outcrops were used from time to time; such as an axe from Natton Hole, Drewsteignton, from a neighbouring outcrop of hornfels, and one from Otterton, east Devon, made of a greenstone localised at Lay Point, St Ives, the sole example of Group II.

The extent to which these axes travelled is well shown by the distribution of Group I (Fig 7). The concentration in Penwith indicates that local needs were first supplied; a few went to communities in mid-Cornwall and south Devon, where one was found at Hazard Hill, but most of the output went to Wessex, from which over sixty axes have been identified. The route evidently was by sea to Dorset, and thence by the Avon to Salisbury Plain, and across Pewsey Vale to the Marlborough Downs. Others went by the Bristol Channel to South Wales, the Mendips and Cotswolds. Finds in Sussex, the lower Thames valley, on the Essex and Yorkshire coasts also indicate long-distance coastal traffic: clearly some of these western Neolithic peoples maintained their practice of sea-voyages long after the immigration. In this connection the discovery of an unusual type of greenstone adze with a quantity of decayed wood thought to be a boat in the Red River gravels at Tuckingmill, Camborne, is significant. Rivers were used to penetrate inland, as is clear from the distribution map (Fig 7).

We can distinguish five early factories, IIA, IV, IVA, XVI and XVII producing axes exclusively. The early Neolithic date for factory IVA was established at Maiden Castle where six specimens were recovered from the occupation of the primary causewayed camp, which was abandoned and built over by a long Bank barrow in late Neolithic times. Other axes from this and the other factories have been found at Hembury and Hazard, both early sites. Most of the exports did not go beyond Somerset, Devon or Dorset but it appears from an axe of Group IIA found at Windmill Hill that some Cornish trade with the central Wessex area was in existence by 2500 BC, which accords with the evidence of the fine exported pottery from the Lizard. The trade must have built up gradually as the population grew, as the coasts became known and the hazards of the long journey overcome.

The later factories are I, IA, III and IIIA, which produced mainly axes, but also axe-hammers, battle-axes, maces and pounders, predominantly for the Wessex market. Several specimens have been found in late Neolithic and Beaker contexts in Wiltshire as at Woodhenge and West Kennet avenue, showing that production continued during the period 2000–1600 BC. The production of the new shaft-holed implements characteristic of the latter part of this epoch shows that the Cornish producers were susceptible to the demands of the new Beaker and Wessex chiefs.

TRACKWAYS

Whilst most long-distance traffic was water-borne, on land well-constructed timber trackways have been found in the Somerset marshes,

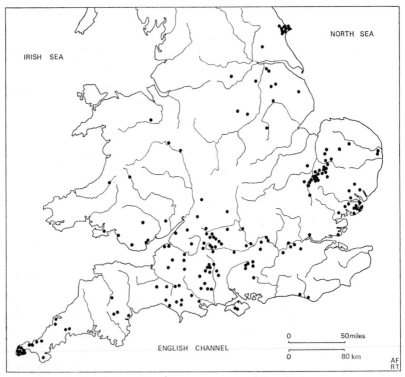

Fig 7 Distribution of Cornish stone axes, group 1, Mount's Bay

primarily to serve the needs of local communities. The tracks were laid on peat containing the remains of woodland trees such as alder, willow and birch which had colonised the earlier reed swamp in the drier conditions of the fourth and third millennium BC and in places on the humified peat of the raised bogs of sphagnum, cotton grass and heathers, which succeeded the fen woodland. One group of tracks, the Honeygore, Honeycat, Bell and the Abbot's Way (Plate 4b) crossed the low-lying ground between the 'islands' of Westhay and Burtle; another, the Blakeway track between Westhay and Wedmore, and a third, a group of thirteen tracks on Chilton moor, seem to be making for the Butterwell valley on the northern side of Polden ridge. Most of the tracks were narrow, 3–4ft wide, and constructed of hazel rods and thin birch timbers laid longitudinally, and supported by more substantial transverse bearers. They are little more than paths, enabling people to penetrate and cross the marshland: the Abbot's Way (Plate 4b) is a more massive track that could have been used for cattle driving or for sledge transport. It was constructed of split alder up to 6ft long laid transversely and held in position by longitudinal birch 'stringers' lashed to numerous long pegs at the side of the track. The pegs had been sharpened before they were driven in by a wooden mallet, like the one of hard yew wood found on Meare Heath in 1971. Radio-carbon dating of the timber shows that trackway construction started about 2800 BC at Honeygore and Chilton but the majority of the tracks date from 2500 BC onwards, with the Bell track and the Abbot's Way the last of the series built about 2000 BC. It is clear from pollen analysis and from chance finds that there was Neolithic settlement around the marshes with forest clearance and some cultivation from the beginning of the third millennium. There would be the attraction of a varied food supply obtainable from the rivers, meres and pools with their fish and wildfowl. The hunter's weapon was a long bow, of which parts of two fine examples have been preserved sunk in the peat on Ashcott and Meare Heaths. Both were of yew wood, 5–6ft long originally, and the Meare bow (Plate 4c) had a decorative binding of leather strips and crossed sinew. The arrow heads were leaf or chisel-shaped finely worked flints, and on analogy with continental survivals mounted in a split shaft with resin gum and bound with sinew.

LATE NEOLITHIC SETTLEMENT

Evidence for late Neolithic settlements in the region is at present derived from surface observations. On the chalk where flint is native to the soil a scatter of flakes and broken implements is not remarkable, but in the west where flint is 'imported' it is significant if dateable artifacts are associated with surface waste. A systematic study of an area near Week on the north-eastern foothills of Dartmoor has demonstrated the existence of sixteen small settlements, occupied intermittently over a long period of time. The sites are by the springheads and extend over a mile and a half of south-facing slopes. The flint waste is concentrated round the spring in patches covering from half to two acres and gradually thinning out. The artifacts collected after ploughing number over 30,000 and were associated with quantities of burnt stones, indicative of cooking and pot-boiling. The sites were first occupied intermittently by Mesolithic hunting groups, who produced pygmy tools, obliquely-blunted, triangular and hollow-based points, blades and gravers and the abundant waste products characteristic of a microlithic industry. Occupation in Neolithic times is indicated by five greenstone axes, one from the Balstone Down factory (Group IV), and by over fifty leaf-shaped and forty transverse (*petit-tranchet* and derivatives) arrowheads. There is also a shale amulet and a mace-hammer, both with an hour-glass perforation made by pecking on both sides of the stone before the art of through drilling with abrasive was mastered. Ripple-flaked plano-convex knives and a few barbed and tanged arrowheads show that the occupation continued into the early Bronze Age. Similar discoveries of surface flints as at Mutters Moor near Sidmouth, at Orleigh near Barnstaple or in the Torbay district show that this open settlement pattern was not uncommon.

We can recognise in such communities the late Neolithic people of the south-west, possessing a stone equipment owing something to both old and new ideas. The flint work with its high proportion of *petit-*

tranchet arrowheads and derivatives reveals a Mesolithic tradition in the population, but the axes and leaf arrowheads are types normal to the primary Neolithic agriculturalists. Without excavation it is impossible to say whether they possessed any pottery that differs from the Hembury–Haldon range. In southern and eastern Britain highly decorated wares were produced by groups with a similar mixed flint industry: both the corded, stamped and pitted Peterborough bowls or the grooved and incised (Rinyo-Clacton) flat-based pots. Isolated specimens of Peterborough ware have been found in Somerset, at Rowbarrow cave on Mendip, at the base of the sphagnum peat on Meare Heath, dating about 2600 BC and at Torbryan caves in south Devon.

RELIGION

For a farming people settling in a virgin land, the need for an increase in their tribe and of their stock was paramount: hence such glimpses as we have of Neolithic cult symbols emphasise this aspect of fertility. A remarkable little image, an hermaphrodite carved in ash wood, with prominent breasts and penis (Plate 4a) was found beneath the Bell trackway at Westhay, Somerset. It had been driven into the ground in a sector where an earlier track had shown weakness and sunk: presumably the god-dolly was intended to invoke supernatural powers for the protection of the new track.

It is likely that some monuments where organised religious activities took place were built by the late Neolithic peoples. These are the henge monuments, embanked arenas with an internal ditch and a single entrance (Atkinson's Class I) at which grooved-ware pottery has frequently been found in southern Britain. Radio-carbon dates indicate that the majority were built about 2000 BC, including the major sites at Durrington Walls and Avebury in Wiltshire, but some small sites such as Llandegai in Caernarvonshire and Arminghall in Norfolk were in use from about 2500 BC. The henges recognised in the south-west are Castilly and Castlewich in east Cornwall and less certainly in the Roseland peninsula and on Parracombe Common, Exmoor. The best preserved is Castilly on Innis Down near Lanivet, which has an oval arena

97 by 161 feet surrounded by a barrier ditch with a broad external bank and an entrance opening north-west; the monument seems designed for ceremonies to be viewed by spectators on the bank. Excavations in 1962 did not produce any dateable finds.

It is not known whether these western henges had a setting of stones or timber posts like most of their southern counterparts, or what is their relationship to the free-standing stone circles on the moors and in the Land's End peninsula. The Stripple Stones circle on Bodmin Moor has a low surrounding bank dug from an external ditch which suggests there was some continuity between the two types of monument and that it remained important to prevent trespass on a sacred enclosure.

To sum up this first phase of colonisation, we have an intrusive people, primarily agriculturalists coming in discrete parties from north-western France, and entering by the southern coasts to settle in the adjacent lowland at the end of the fourth and the early third millenniums. They exploited the various metamorphic rocks for material for the stone axes they needed in clearing the woodland and for cultivation and built up gradually a flourishing trade with their contemporaries in southern Britain. The distribution shows that these early communities were few and, apart from the Land's End peninsula, the land was sparsely settled.

CHAPTER III

The Tomb Builders

So far as is known at present, no burial places can be specifically connected with the early Neolithic people in Devon or Cornwall. There are no earthen long barrows in east Devon, where in the absence of suitable building stone they might be expected, and it must be concluded that for the inhabitants of Hembury, High Peak and Haldon the preservation of the bones of their ancestors was not important. There are several ways of disposal of the dead that leave no trace, such as exposure to beasts and birds of prey, or throwing the bones into the sea or rivers; it must also be remembered that isolated burials or piles of bones would leave no archaeological trace in the acid greensand soils after 4,000 years.

The impetus to build the great stone tombs to be described in this chapter was localised and was probably due to new arrivals in Cornwall and south-west Devon with a similar stone economy and way of life, but with a different religious belief, in which the prosperity of the community was dependent on the spirits of the dead in a nearby tomb or temple. Elsewhere the sacred character of the tomb is made explicit by a crudely carved life-size figure of a female deity, as at Four Knocks in Ireland or Barclodiad y Gawres in North Wales.

The development of communal tomb building in stone is a phenomenon common to the western seaboards of Britain and Ireland throughout Neolithic times and is manifest as well on the Atlantic coasts of France, Portugal and Spain extending into the western Mediterranean. It is still uncertain how or where the idea originated: radio-carbon

47

dates indicate that certain tombs in Brittany and in Ireland were in existence a little before 3000 BC, which is earlier than any yet known farther south. Similar early dates have been obtained for some earthen long barrows containing communal burials in timber structures in southern and eastern England. It would appear that more than one centre was involved and that the concept and building techniques spread amongst existing agricultural communities, assisted by trading contacts and sea voyages during the third millennium BC.

The new stone tombs were family vaults, spaciously and elaborately constructed for successive burials. The funeral rites included the lighting of fires and the digging of small pits to receive libations, funeral feasts and animal sacrifices, and a ceremonial blocking of the entrance to the tomb after each interment. The labour, skill, and care devoted by a primitive people to the construction of these tombs shows the importance that the ancestral dead had attained in their thoughts.

Broadly speaking, the tombs can be divided into Gallery Graves, elongated rectangular tombs as the name implies, entered directly, and usually covered by a long mound, and Passage Graves, in which the tomb chamber is usually sub-circular and approached by a passage leading in from the edge of a round mound or cairn.

It is generally agreed that three main centres of tomb building can be distinguished in western Britain: the Severn–Cotswold group of Gallery Graves in south Wales and Gloucestershire; the Clyde–Carlingford group in south-west Scotland and Northern Ireland; later builders of Passage Graves came to eastern and southern Ireland (the Boyne group) and from these, expansion and a secondary colonisation of the coastlands bordering the Irish Sea took place during the second half of the third millennium. In the process, the tomb architecture was modified and both elaborate and degenerate forms were evolved, so that in some late examples, it is hard to perceive their origin or affinities.

In the south-west four classes of tombs can be distinguished, all built of large stones, mainly granite, from which the modern generic name, *megalith*, is derived, which has replaced the former Celtic *cromlech* or *dolmen*. They are (i) Gallery Graves with simple rectangular tomb-chambers, terminally situated in long or oval mounds or cairns; (ii) Penwith tombs, similar squarish chambers, closed or with a restricted entry and covered by a round cairn; (iii) one example of a Passage Grave; and (iv) Entrance Graves, which are gallery-like chambers placed at the end of a round mound, and are derivatives of Passage Graves. Such divisions, based on the present appearance of the tombs, are rather arbitrary because many of the cairns are denuded, the structures ruinous and their contents have been removed, lost and ill-recorded. Very little modern excavation has taken place and that only of tombs that were almost totally destroyed, so that detailed information about the funeral rites is lacking.

The distribution (Fig 8) is coastal with a concentration in the case of classes ii and iv in the Land's End peninsula. Entry of immigrants by the Camel estuary on the north coast is indicated by some of the Gallery Graves, whilst others landing on the south coast penetrated to the edge

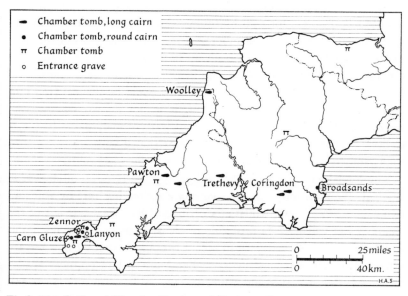

Fig 8 Distribution of Chamber Tombs and Entrance Graves

of Dartmoor, but not into east Devon. Most of the tombs are inconspicuously sited, on hillsides and the edges of plateau country, and in the case of the Entrance Graves at Pennance and Brane even in a little valley. It may be surmised that these places were chosen because they were close to the settlements. Some, however, are crest-sited; the long mound of Corringdon Ball, South Brent, is on a saddle at 1100ft between the Avon and its tributary, the Glaze brook, and though concealed when approached along the ridge, is dominant on the skyline when seen from the west across the brook. Such sites probably were chosen because they were conspicuous in the view of the living.

GALLERY GRAVES

These tombs are characterised by a long or oval mound, of which the best preserved are at Pawton (Plate 3a), Corringdon Ball and Woolley, standing 4, 6 and 12 feet high respectively. At Lanivet, Trethevy and Lanyon, the cairns are only just discernible because material has been removed by farmers for wall building, whilst Spintser's Rock, Drewsteignton and Carwynnen, Camborne, have been wholly denuded. Normally the mound or cairn was built up to the level of the chamber and functioned as a ramp up which the heavy capstones were dragged on rollers, and as a platform from which they could be manoeuvred into position. Lacking modern excavation, it is not known whether the cairns were built with internal revetment walls or marginal slabs (peristalith), or whether any of them were constructed with a fore-court to the chamber, as is usual in Gallery Graves in the Cotswolds.

The tomb chambers have also suffered by the removal of stones: at Lanivet, Bodmin, only the great capstone measuring 10ft by 16ft and two supporters remain, whilst at Corringdon Ball what was left of the chamber has collapsed in a tumble of slabs. Lanyon, Carwynnen and Spintsers' Rock also collapsed in recent times and what we now see are nineteenth-century reconstructions. The tomb at Pawton, near Wadebridge is better preserved and would repay scientific excavation (Plate 3a). The closed chamber, half-full of soil, is towards the broad end of the

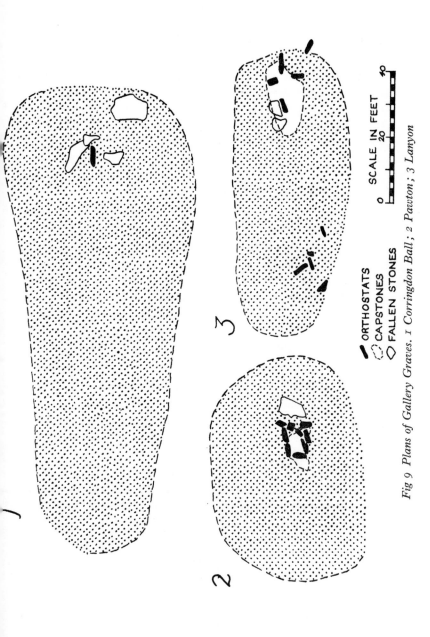

Fig 9 *Plans of Gallery Graves. 1 Corringdon Ball; 2 Pawton; 3 Lanyon*

SCALE IN FEET

0   20   40

ORTHOSTATS
CAPSTONES
FALLEN STONES

70ft oval mound. It is covered by a thick level capstone 10ft long by 7ft wide, now bearing on three of the seven uprights that constitute the chamber; formerly the capstone was 3ft longer, a piece having cracked off and fallen forwards; when unbroken it would have rested on two other half-buried uprights which, with the front supporter, formed in effect a shallow façade in front of the closed chamber. This is an important feature because it links this Cornish megalith with others in the south, such as Pentre Ifan in Pembrokeshire, or the Grey Mare and Colts in west Dorset, both tombs with a shallow crescentic façade in front of a closed chamber.

Trethevy, St Cleer, south of Bodmin Moor also has a closed chamber covered by a sloping capstone, but with side stones that project forwards to form an antechamber in the manner of an Irish 'portal-dolmen'. The entrance to the inner tomb was by a small aperture in the bottom corner of the enormous granite slab that divides it from the antechamber, through which it is just possible to crawl. A restricted entry to megalithic tombs is not uncommon, reflecting the natural desire of a primitive people to keep the spirits of the dead in the tomb, despite the difficulties of inserting fresh bodies for burial when the occasion arose. Devices vary for narrowing the entry; some, like Trethevy, utilise natural cleavage or introduce small blocking stones, but in some tombs, not confined to any one class, a round hole was laboriously pecked out of a slab. Two of these so-called 'portholes' are found in Cornwall, though neither tomb has survived: the Men-an-Tol, Madron and the Tolvaen at Gweek, both worked in the granite.

There is no evidence from grave-goods for the date or cultural affinities of the south-western Gallery Graves. The only indication that they were built for inhumations, and therefore of early origin, comes from West Lanyon, a tomb now practically destroyed but found intact about 1800. The 13ft capstone had apparently slipped during construction and then had been covered by the mound. Digging in the chamber produced half a skull, thigh bones and other human bones, 'lying in a promiscuous state and a disordered manner', and above them 'a broken urn with ashes', presumably a Bronze Age cremation succeeding the

5a *(above)* Three beakers found with inhumations in the Wick barrow, Stoguersey, Somerset. Heights 7in, 6·3in and 6in. Taunton Museum
5b *(below left)* Handled beaker from Try, Gulval, Cornwall. Height 6·3in. Truro Museum 5c *(below right)* Food-vessel, southern type, from Broad Down, Farway, East Devon. Height 5in. Exeter Museum

6a *(above)* Stone circle at Tregaseal, St Just, West Cornwall
6b *(below)* Stone rows at Shovel Down, Chagford, Dartmoor

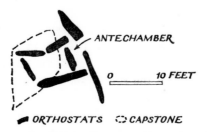

Fig 10 Plan of the tomb chamber at Zennor Quoit, west Cornwall

primary collective burials. For although W. C. Borlase held that the bones belonged to a single inhumation, it is now recognised that disarticulate and disordered bones are characteristic of successive or collective interments, being the remains of earlier burials that have been pushed aside or rearranged to make room for a later one.

PENWITH TOMBS

The Penwith tombs are smaller monuments: the remains of their circular cairns range from 32 to 40 feet in diameter and the chambers, though covered by large capstones, are not much bigger than large cists. Like Trethevy and Pawton, the chamber was closed by a large slab at the time of construction, making it difficult to insert additional burials. The tombs are all conspicuously sited above the 400ft contour on the little hills of the Land's End peninsula. It is unfortunate that the only recent excavation was at Sperris Quoit, Zennor, a tomb that had been ruined in antiquity: the only significant discovery was a dedicatory pit containing some burnt bone and charcoal.

Of the four other examples, Zennor Quoit (Plate 3b) is the most interesting structurally and archaeologically, though the monument now differs from its original form. In the eighteenth century when William Borlase drew it, the 18ft capstone was horizontal; its present tilt is due to the removal of supporters to make a nearby cart-shed. Like Trethevy, Zennor has an antechamber formed by projecting side-supporters and by two fine slabs set up with their outer faces at right angles to the long axis of the chamber (Fig 10), a dignified façade confronting those who approached the tomb. There is a small space between the uprights to enter the antechamber but the main chamber is closed. Some casual digging in the main chamber by R. J. Noall in 1910 produced some cremated bones, a flint scraper and flakes, the remains of a small bi-conical pot (Fig 11) and the rim of another decorated with diagonal incisions. Previously, in 1881, a farmer named Grenfell and his son had delved under the paving in the antechamber, breaking up two slabs by blasting and finding a perforated whetstone (Fig 12) of a type found in early Bronze Age graves in Wessex. Part of a third pot with cord ornament also probably came to light on this occasion. Both groups of finds can now be recognised as of Bronze Age date: the incised ware has analogies in domestic pottery from Gwithian (layer 5) and from Dartmoor, and the biconical pot with others in Scilly. If the evidence of the whetstone be accepted, it appears that Zennor Quoit was in use until about 1600–1500 BC. This need not surprise us for whilst the antechamber with its façade link it with the Gallery Graves and with the Irish portal-dolmens, the round mound which survives at other Penwith tombs indicates contact with the Passage Graves and their late derivatives, the Entrance Graves.

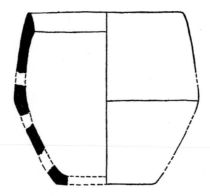

Fig 11 Small bi-conical pot from Zennor Quoit, west Cornwall (reconstructed from fragments by Bernard Wailes)

Fig 12 Whetstone from Zennor Quoit, west Cornwall. Original 3¼in long

PASSAGE GRAVES

There is only one tomb in the south-west that has claims to be recognised as a Passage Grave: the wrecked chamber and denuded cairn at Broadsands, Paignton. It is sited on the south-facing slopes above a sandy inlet on Torbay and within easy reach of a tract of open limestone country. Excavations by C. A. R. Radford showed that the chamber was polygonal, built of eleven small orthostats, 3–5ft high, with the interstices filled with dry-stone walling, and roofed by a single slab. It was entered on one side of the chamber by a very narrow passage built of small stones throughout; the cairn was probably circular, and 40ft in diameter. The tomb has apparently been used over a period of time: the latest burial was a flexed inhumation of a young adult male with which was associated a collared rim sherd of decorated late Neolithic pottery; of the earlier burials only a few bones belonging to two adult males and an infant were found trodden into the floor of the chamber. With these were fragments of western Neolithic pottery, including some from carinated bowls like those from Carn Brea. It was apparent that the first burials in the tomb had been cleared away, purifying fires had then been lit and the chamber roughly paved, before the last body had been placed in the tomb.

The indications are that this tomb with its two periods of inhumations is of early date, despite its small size and poor construction. This accords with the Breton evidence where radio-carbon dates of 3270 and 3390 BC have been obtained from Île Carn and Île Bono (Les Sept Îles), both passage graves on islands off the northern coast. Radford indeed has claimed that it is directly related to the classic Pavia type of Iberian tomb, such as Alcarapinha I, Alentejo, in central Portugal. Analogies with some Passage Graves in north-western France, with Parc Guren I in the Morbihan, with Pleneuf in the Côtes du Nord and with La Sergenté in Jersey have also been suggested, though these are all much more imposing structures, the products of well-established communities. The builders of Broadsands can best be regarded as some bold voyagers who out-distanced their contemporaries and were alone in gaining a foothold on the southern coast of Devon.

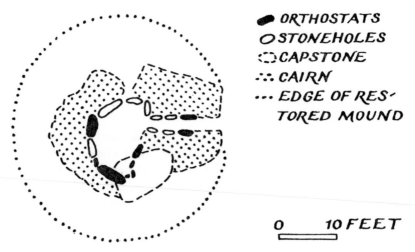

ORTHOSTATS
STONEHOLES
CAPSTONE
CAIRN
EDGE OF RES-
TORED MOUND

0   10 FEET

Fig 13 Plan of the Broadsands passage grave, Devon

ENTRANCE GRAVES

The other group of people who have claims to be of Passage Grave descent are the builders of the Entrance Graves in Penwith. The tombs are all very similar: there is no passage and the narrow rectangular chamber with a ceiling of flat slabs, like a stone cupboard, is entered directly at the edge of a small conical mound, 15–25ft in diameter, 6–10ft high, which has a conspicuous kerb of large boulders. Good examples can be seen at Treen, Pennance and Brane in the Land's End peninsula. Many others are found in the Scilly Isles, the granite archipelago situated 28 miles out in the Atlantic, and there can be little doubt that it was from here that the colonists came to the mainland. At this time the Scillies were one island with a coast line approximating to the present 10 fathom line and consequently there was more cultivable flat land available to support the population. Other tombs of this kind are found in Ireland, two near the cemetery of great passage graves on the Boyne, at Knowth and Townley Hall, and another group of five or six round Tramore in County Waterford. A few occur in the Channel Islands such as la Trépied, Guernsey. The Townley Hall tomb is of particular interest since it was built over a Neolithic habitation affording evidence of its late date.

In the Scillies there is evidence of the formal development of these tombs and of their use and date. In the earliest examples on St Mary's, an upright slab marks the division between the passage and the chamber, and in another, Bants Carn, the entry to the chamber is shown by projecting slabs in the side walls of the passage, which are the ends of an interior encircling revetment wall. In the later examples, the division between passage and tomb has disappeared and we are left with the Entrance Grave, which confusingly looks like a covered gallery and was so referred to by Hencken.

The tombs initially were built to contain inhumations, for 'skeletal debris' was found in the floor of Obadiah's barrow on Gugh in 1900 but most held inurned cremations placed successively in the tomb. At Knackyboy on St Martin's, no less than twenty-two urns were recovered from about half of one of these graves, the other half having been previously rifled. The first interments in decorated biconical urns were set in hollows on the roughly paved floor and ashes from the pyre heaped over them; later, straight-sided urns were placed on top of them so that the low vault was filled nearly to the roof with tiers of crushed and broken pots. In the ashes associated with the first cremations were eight blue glass beads and one star-shaped bead of faience, an exotic type that can be dated to the Middle Bronze Age, c 1300 BC. The forms of both types of urns are Bronze Age and there can be little doubt that Scillonian Entrance Graves were being used until a late date, perhaps until 1000 BC. Nevertheless they are collective tombs, very different from the single graves normal in the Bronze Age and in this sense their builders must be regarded as a megalithic people, even though they were using bronze for their tools and weapons; isolated in the islands, they were conservative of the old rites and beliefs concerning the dead.

None of the urn burials from the mainland have survived—the cupboards are bare—but here too the form of tomb persisted to a late date with the cairn enlarged and conspicuously sited on hilltops in the customary Bronze Age manner. At Tregaseal, St Just, a perforated whetstone similar to that from Zennor Quoit (Fig 12) was found with cremated bones and pottery, since lost, on the floor of the tomb in the centre of a large oval cairn: a secondary cremation was in an adjoining cist, placed in a large ribbon-handled urn (p 91): both burials should date from the early Middle Bronze Age, c 1500–1300 BC. At Carn Gluze, a great walled cairn on the cliffs at St Just, a typical Entrance Grave in the outer perimeter clearly was later than the corbelled structure in the centre of the cairn which contained at least one small pot of Middle Bronze Age type.

Carn Gluze is a very remarkable structure: it was excavated in 1874 by W. C. Borlase and a gang of local miners, and although many details of construction have been lost, the plans made by W. C. Lukis are informative (Plate 2). In the light of recent knowledge, the following sequence can be deduced (Fig 14). The primary construction was a T-shaped pit (1), which was excavated 7ft deep in the rocky subsoil and entered by rough steps cut in its sloping shaft; it contained only greasy

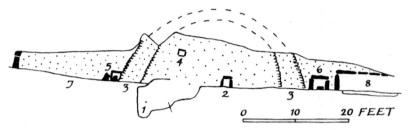

Fig 14 Reconstructed section of Carn Gluze, St Just, west Cornwall (after W. C. Lukis). 1, primary pit: 2, four cists; 3, domed cairn; 4–6, cists; 7, cairn ring; 8, entrance grave

mould in which a stone bead or amulet was found. The pit may have held an inhumation burial, the bones having dissolved in the acid soil, or more likely, it was a sacred pit, a symbolic entry to the underworld. Round the top of the pit-shaft there were four small cists (2) surrounded by remains of burning and containing miniature pots, one a bucket-shaped urn of late Middle Bronze Age form. These probably held offerings of food or drink, since only two minute pieces of bone were found in them. The second construction was an oval double-walled cairn (3) 30ft by 37ft with a domed surface and still surviving to a height of 12ft. Its two walls, which are 5ft apart and which pass over the primary pit, were corbelled inwards and the space between loosely filled with pitched slabs. At the same time, the little cists were covered with stones, which helped to support the corbelled revetment walls of the rising dome. When this packing was 5ft deep, another cist (4) was built containing pottery and the bones of a lamb, probably a final offering to the spirits of the underworld. There was no entry to the dome; but at the base of the outer wall, Borlase found a spread of charcoal and two more empty cists (5–6), one covered by tilted slabs. Finally the dome itself was encased by a massive cairn-ring (7) 18–20ft wide, 4–5ft high and walled externally. The Entrance Grave (8) was built in the south-west segment of the cairn-ring, more or less on the same axis as the shaft to the original pit, and in a line with one of the external cists. It alone was in contact with the outside world; quantities of burnt human bones and broken potsherds were found beneath its paved floor, though the last interments in the chamber had disappeared. Its marginal position is significant; at Carn Gluze this tomb is external to a concealed sacred place, in which an underworld cult had been practised in all probability.

Something similar can be seen in a Bronze Age turf barrow at Six-wells, Glamorgan, but on a much smaller scale; this had a ritual pit in the centre, a hole only 9 inches in diameter, an enclosure marked by a circle of stakes and a cremation in a cist on its margin. The double-walled dome at Carn Gluze, however, has a megalithic ancestry: analogous dry-stone structures can be seen in the long cairns of some Severn–Cotswold Gallery Graves, namely the drum-like 'rotunda' covering a cist in the centre of the cairn at Notgrove, and the double-walled structure at Ty-Isaf, Breconshire,which surrounded the principal transepted chamber at the tail-end of the cairn. A relationship can also be perceived with the concentric revetment walls in the round cairns of the large corbel-vaulted passage graves in Brittany, such as Île Longue or Er Mané de Queric at Carnac.

It must be concluded that in default of modern excavation relatively little is known about the builders of the Neolithic tombs in the south-west. Judging from the surviving remains this was not an area where the cult of the ancestral dead reached a high pitch: there are no symbolic carvings as on the Boyne or in North Wales, and no large or complex monuments comparable with the transepted gallery-graves of Severn–Cotswold region or the Irish court cairns. The south-western people were content with a modest achievement; with cairns that rarely exceed 70ft in length or in diameter, and with single small chambers usually closed or with a restricted entry, perhaps simply built as ossuaries; only in the selection of the capstone and in the frontal arrangements have the tombs any architectural pretensions.

CHAPTER IV

The Beaker and Food-Vessel Peoples

The beginning of the second millennium BC saw another element added to the already mixed Neolithic population in the south-west; a small group of the dynamic Beaker folk, whose advent paved the way for the development of Bronze Age society in this region as elsewhere in Britain. They were of continental origin, originally from Spain but spreading rapidly north and east, on the one hand by sea to north-west France and on the other overland to central Europe, Germany and the Netherlands. They were physically distinct from the Neolithic stocks, a race of powerfully built, short, ugly men and women, with round heads and prominent brow-ridges. They differed fundamentally from their predecessors in their burial rite, which was individual interment, usually under a small round cairn, instead of in a communal tomb. The assertion of the individual in this way in place of the ancestral family group implies a major re-orientation in society. Their basic possessions were those of the bowman, a figure skilled both as warrior and hunter like the dreaded North American Indian. Their wooden bows and quivers have perished but their barbed flint arrowheads, and hunters' knives of copper or of flint survive in the graves. Such equipment implies a different way of life from that of the settled Neolithic cultivators; it explains their great mobility and the rapidity with which they established their ascendancy. In central Europe, they participated in the winning and working of copper and there is little doubt that they were instrumental in spreading the knowledge and techniques of the new metallurgy.

Their name, as is well known, is derived from their characteristic pottery vessel, the beaker, made of highly ornamented thin red ware, which owes its colour and texture to skilled firing at a high temperature, probably in some form of kiln, with a forced draught, a technique acquired for smelting. From variations in the shapes, and the style and motifs of pottery decoration, together with the associated grave-goods, it has been possible to identify several intrusive groups in Britain, and their continental sources. The first people who crossed the North Sea between 2000 and 1800 BC were makers of what is termed by David Clarke the European Bell beaker (E). There are pots with a characteristic smooth profile, like a *campanula* flower. The earliest types were decorated by winding a length of tightly twisted cord or sinew spirally round the pot when the clay was wet (All-over-cord beakers). The majority of Bell beakers, however, were decorated with a toothed comb, producing a hyphenated line, or with incisions, arranged in horizontal zones. Later immigrants, from the Middle Rhine, with metal-working equipment settled in Wessex initially (W/MR beakers), whilst others from the Netherlands populated the north-east coasts, including Scotland (N/MR and N/NR). Subsequent expansion and mixing of these closely related groups resulted in the development between 1700 and 1600 BC of British styles of beakers, with distinctive regional variations, Southern (S), Northern (N) and East Anglian (E Ang) as defined by Clarke.

The south-west was remote from the main migration streams and the areas of primary colonisation, and received its population late and from insular sources, mainly Wessex (Fig 15). Two elements can be recognised: first derivatives of the European Bell beaker, with the characteristic simple zonal patterns as from Langcombe in the Plym valley, and secondly varieties of the developed southern British types previously known as long-necked beakers. These have a well-marked constriction or waist between the tall splayed neck and the rounded lower body and in our region are characterised by bold schemes of geometric decoration featuring lozenge and bar-chevron motifs, as at Wick, Somerset (Plate 5a). There is also a beaker decorated in the Northern insular style from Culbone, Somerset, and one with the barbed-wire type of decoration from Chagford, Dartmoor, in which a jagged line was produced by winding thread around a sliver of bone or flint and impressing the spool on the wet pot. The varieties were in contemporary use in the south-west, as was revealed in the grave mound at Wick, near Stogursey on the north Somerset coast. This was a large barrow, 90ft in diameter, 10ft high, excavated in 1907 by H. St George Gray. The soil casing concealed a walled cairn, 27ft across, beneath which a number of skeletons had been laid on the old ground surface and which had been disturbed by tomb robbers, surprisingly in Roman times. The three Beaker burials were secondaries, inserted high up in the rubble of the primary cairn. Each was a contracted inhumation, a man with legs tightly drawn up and arms bent; the first was buried with a Bell beaker, the second with a long-necked (S3) beaker with chevron decoration and a flint knife-dagger, and the third with a long-necked beaker with lozenge decoration (S2), some flints and a pebble hammer. There can be little

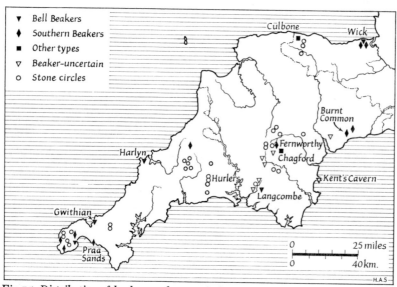

Fig 15 Distribution of beakers and stone circles

doubt that the vessels are approximately contemporary, the products of wide-ranging communities who returned from hunting grounds on the Quantocks to use the barrow built on the coast as their cemetery. The close parallels of the bar-chevron necked beaker with others in the Vale of Glamorgan indicates that some of these people crossed the Channel to colonise the opposite coast. The distribution in the south-west (Fig 15) shows a concentration in the Land's End peninsula and on Dartmoor, and some in east Devon and on the Bristol Channel coast.

The burials were almost all in cists, just large enough to hold the trussed bodies, as can be seen in the Culbone cist from Exmoor in the Taunton Museum. Some cists are so small, like the 2ft by 2½ft stone box on Trevedra Common, St Just, that they can only have held the body of a child or a cremation. The burials were covered by a small round cairn or mound, 12ft to 20ft in diameter, rarely more than 2ft high and inconspicuously sited on moorland slopes. An exception is the burial recently excavated by Mrs S. Pollard on Burnt Common, near Ottery St Mary, east Devon, where the inhumation was in a shallow grave lined with chert. It was surrounded by a ring built of small stones 5ft wide and 3ft high, at a distance of 15ft from the grave. There were two small pits within the cairn-ring containing some charcoal, probably taken from a ceremonial fire that had preceded the building of the cairn-ring. The beaker, a late Southern variety (S4) with cordons and irregular incisions, had lain on its side in the grave, with two fossil sea-urchins as the only other grave-goods.

In other burials grave-goods were also poor and scanty: a bronze blade and a V-perforated lignite button at Fernworthy, barbed and tanged arrowheads at Langcombe and Lakehead, and a bracer at Archerton are all from Dartmoor. The beakers include a few decorative long-necked southern types, as at Wick and Fernworthy, but in others there is a tendency to thicken the rim or to add a moulding below it, as in the handled example from Try, Gulval. A date about 1600 BC is indicated for most of them.

The few known settlements are coastal: at Praa Sands, Marazion, where a long-necked beaker (S2) was recovered from a midden, at Gwithian and Harlyn Bay on the north Cornish coast and perhaps also at Kent's Cavern, Torquay. Only at Gwithian is there any evidence of structure, where two successive timber houses have been identified by Professor C. Thomas, the earlier with a central post, the later qval with a porch set within a rectangular palisaded enclosure. Sherds of Bell beaker were associated with pottery decorated with plaited cord in the early Bronze Age manner. Some grain was grown on the evidence of saddle querns.

In their later stages, the Beaker folk in the south-west associated with the makers of the southern type of food-vessel, and adopted the rite of cremation. These food-vessels are unpretentious small pots of biconical form, with bevelled rim and occasional ornament of whipped or twisted cord: it is not clear how they originated in our area, but a late Neolithic ancestry may be presumed. Their cultural context is known only from burials. At Broad Down, on the greensand plateau of east Devon, a cremation with a developed southern beaker (S2) was inserted into the edge of a small cairn of flints, which covered a primary cremation in an inverted food-vessel (Plate 5c). At Charmy Down, near Bath, an in- humation with a necked-beaker (S2) a bronze knife-dagger, and a ribbed shale bead was contemporary with a cremation in a food-vessel in the centre of a walled cairn like that at Wick, whilst at Cataclews, Harlyn Bay, another food-vessel of this type was associated with a stone battle- axe, a weapon frequently deposited with necked-beakers.

At Tregulland, on Wilsey Down flanking Bodmin Moor, a food- vessel cremation was the last interment in a complex barrow structure, succeeding both the cremation of an archer with two barbed arrowheads, one tanged, one hollow-based, and the primary inhumation, which un- fortunately had been thoroughly disturbed. Skilled excavation by Paul Ashbee, however, showed how rich and varied were the funeral rites and customs now developing amongst these peoples. The primary burial was set apart, enclosed by two circles of close-set stakes 14 and 24ft in diameter: the cremation with arrowheads was placed in an elongated grave and fires had been lit in a shallow pit, both just outside the stake circles. The stakes had then been removed and replaced by a cairn-ring, walled internally, and incorporating a number of cup-marked slabs of the local slate. These circular pecked hollows appear to be protective symbols for the Food-Vessel people, analogous to the *occuli* or eye symbols of the Passage Grave people. At Tregulland the food-vessel cremation was placed on the ground within the cairn-ring, and the whole centre was then filled up with soil dug from an encircling ditch, to make a barrow 30ft in diameter.

Other rites unconnected with any burials were in evidence on Farway Hill, east Devon, which had taken place within two small flint cairn-rings. They involved the digging of numerous small pits and holes, 141 in all, varying from 6ins to 7ft long and from 6ins to 30ins deep. Some contained charcoal, one with some burnt bone, and these perhaps were dug to receive the remains of burnt offerings; others had a clean filling and may have been dug for libations. Since some pits were found beneath the cairn-rings, it is evident that these circular enclosures were erected after the rites had begun. There is little doubt that this was a sacred place, and on analogy with the burial on nearby Burnt Common (p. 66), it probably belonged to the Beaker folk. The phenomenon is repeated in later Bronze Age ritual barrows (p. 127).

STONE ROWS

The 'single graves' of the Beaker and Food-Vessel peoples were concealed generally by an inconspicuous small mound. An interesting local development of this very simple funeral monument occurs on Dartmoor, where some 60 little cairns have settings of rows of stones. A characteristic example is on Watern Down, near the Warren House Inn, where a double row of fifty pairs of granite uprights extends for 180 yards from a transverse terminal slab (the so-called 'blocking stone') up a gentle slope to a low cairn 20ft in diameter. The stones vary in size from a foot high, just visible in the heather, to nearly 6 feet, the largest being nearest the cairn, as also in the Down Tor and one of the Shovel Down rows. Two shapes are significant, a pillar and a triangular-topped slab; at Merrivale, these two forms are paired as terminals to the

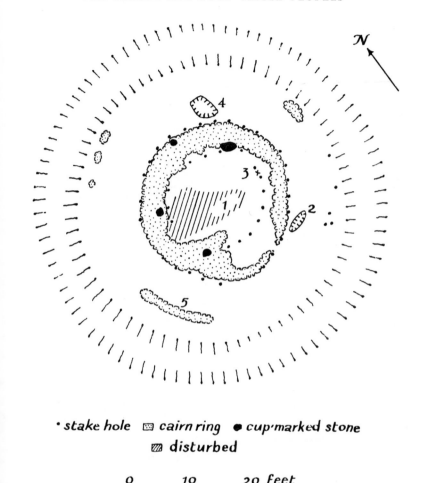

· stake hole ⊞ cairn ring ● cup·marked stone
▨ disturbed

0   10   20 feet

Fig 16 Plan of Tregulland barrow, Cornwall. 1 disturbed primary burial; 2 crema-
tion grave; 3 food-vessel cremation; 4 'ritual' pit; 5 remnant of outer kerb

southern row; at Shovel Down, Chagford, they head the row beside
the cairn. There is no consistency in the orientation of the alignments,
the direction being in nearly every case related to an upward slope to the
burial place. In several instances, as at Harter on the Meavy, the rows

69

are associated with running water and lead up from the banks of the stream to the cairn. There is usually only space for one person, or at most two, to walk between the rows, and since the small cairn is invariably approached uphill, its height is enhanced because it is seen on a false crest (Plate 6b). The alignments thus provide a dignified approach to the burial place.

The cairns usually have a kerb or a circle of upright slabs (a peristalith) on their circumference and a central cist. At Shovel Down (Fig 18) and Yellowmead, Sheepstor, there are four concentric circles of upright stones within the cairn, perhaps the equivalent of the concentric stake circles discovered at Tregulland.

It was unfortunate that in the only recent excavation of a stone row at Cholwichtown, Lee Moor in 1961, the large burial pit had been disturbed: it was surrounded by a free-standing circle of eight uprights, 16ft in diameter. Despite careful stripping of the entire row of ninety-one stones, nothing was found to date or to explain the monument.

Not every row is associated with a cairn: on Headland Warren, Challacombe, three rows converge on a standing stone, and at Merrivale, Princetown, the northern double row has a blocking stone as its terminal. Whether such stones were sacred in themselves like a totem-pole, or whether they mark a burial place, as some menhirs do in Cornwall, has not been ascertained.

Two rows in the Erme Valley are of exceptional length (Fig 17). The row on Butterdon Hill starts from a cairn 35ft in diameter with a conspicuous peristalith and extends for over a mile along the 1,250 foot hill-top. The Stall Moor row starts from a free-standing stone circle 50ft in diameter, possibly but not certainly sepulchral in origin, and continues at 1,200ft for over half a mile before it descends steeply to the river: some of the small stones are covered in blanket peat showing that the monument was built before the Sub-Atlantic deterioration of the climate after 900 BC. Across the river, the alignment continues upstream just above the valley floor for another half-mile to a tributary, the Red Lake stream whence it can be traced intermittently up the slopes of Greenhill and fading out just before it reaches a small barrow on the

7a *(above left)* Gold cup from an early Bronze Age burial at Rillaton, Linkinhorne, East Cornwall. Height 3·3in. British Museum 7b *(above right)* Shale cup from Broad Down, Farway, East Devon. Height 3·7in. Exeter Museum 7c *(below)* Bronzed dagger, pygmy cup and shale bead necklace from Stevenstone, Upton Pyne, Exeter. Dagger 3·8in; cup, height 1·3in. Exeter Museum

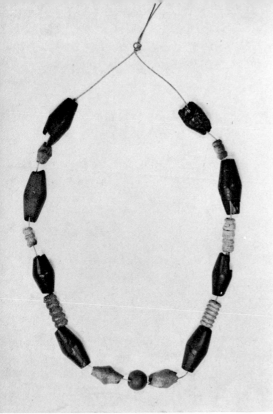

8a *(left)* Necklace of shale, amber and faience beads, from a cremation at Bamfylde Hill, North Molton, Devon. Exeter Museum
8b *(below)* Gold *lunulae* from Harlyn Bay, St Merryn, Cornwall. Diameter 8·3in and 8·6in. Truro Museum

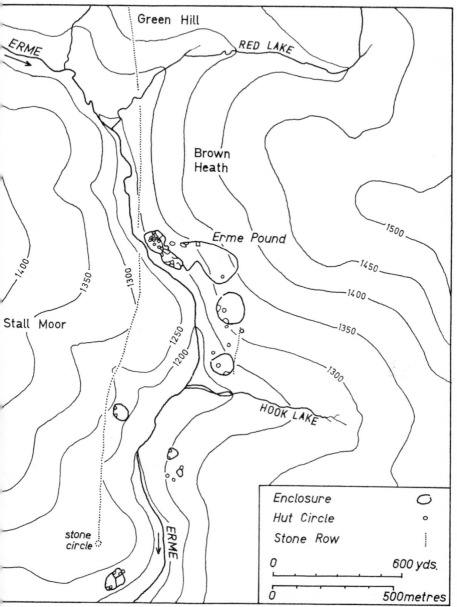

Fig 17 *Map of Erme valley, Dartmoor, showing the long stone row on Stall Moor*

crest at 1,550 feet; a distance in all of two and a quarter miles. There is no indication whether the whole thing is one setting or whether two have coalesced.

These long rows must have had a rather different purpose from the general run of stone-lined paths to the tombs. They are unlikely to mark tribal divisions of grazing, as their course does not follow a natural boundary and their ends are not secured. Contemporary monuments of comparable length are the West Kennet stone avenue linking two sacred sites, Avebury and the Sanctuary, the embanked avenue which leads from Stonehenge to the River Avon, and the long embanked enclosures known as a Cursus, for example at Stonehenge and Gussage Down, Dorset. The function of the Cursus is unknown but an attractive conjecture, originating with the eighteenth-century antiquary William Stukeley, is that they mark an arena for funeral games and races. It is conceivable that the long rows on Dartmoor mark a course followed by runners, like those at the Grasmere Fell sports today, or by a religious procession.

SANCTUARIES

It is evident that certain places on Dartmoor acquired a special sanctity amongst these people and were used for burials and for ceremonial by several generations. At centres like Shovel Down (Fig 18), Fernworthy, Merrivale or Drizzlecombe, two, three or even four rows with their cairns are associated with other cairns, cists, standing stones *(menhirs)* or with a small-scale free-standing circle, the whole group extending over a considerable tract of moorland. It is not unreasonable to assume that the monuments in these sanctuaries are, broadly speaking, contemporary. The few finds are significantly of the Beaker period: a developed Southern beaker (S2) from a small cairn at Fernworthy, scraps of another from a cist in the Drizzlecombe group, and a 'barbed wire' beaker from a small cairn near the row on Watern Down, Chagford. Moreover, the only close parallel in Britain to the Dartmoor rows—the cairn at Garrywhin in Caithness, on which six rows of small stones converge, leading up to it from a nearby stream—contained an inhumation

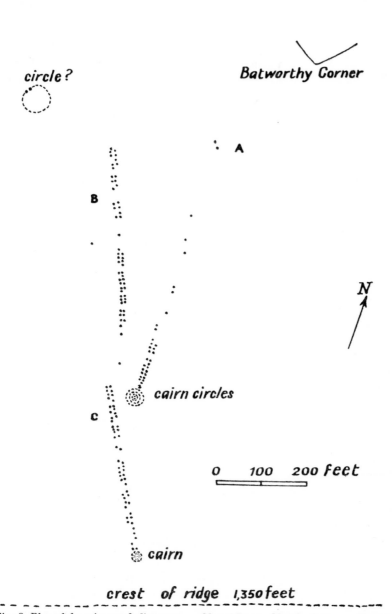

circle?

Batworthy Corner

A

B

N

cairn circles

C

0   100   200 feet

cairn

crest of ridge 1,350 feet

Fig 18 Plan of the cairns and alignments on Shovel Down, Chagford, Devon. Row A is over 550ft long, row B 476ft and row C 375ft

with a cord-ornamented beaker in a cist. Similarly in Holland where the timber equivalent to a stone row has been found at Zeijen, in Drenthe, the indications are that it is of early Bronze Age date. Here a double line of postholes, 120ft long and 5ft wide, begins with a blocking post and leads to a turf barrow, which covered four inhumations and a square mortuary house set within a double circle of posts. It is likely that the custom of erecting timber alignments for a ceremonial approach was not uncommon in Britain but has only rarely been detected in excavation. Postholes for an avenue were found by G. Wainwright at Durrington Walls, Wiltshire; it marked the approach to the Northern Circle, probably a roofed ceremonial house, one of several within the huge embanked henge monument, which was in use from about 2000–1600 BC. Like the Dartmoor examples, the avenue leads up an incline.

Stone circles were also build independently of burials on the high moorlands (Fig 15), on Exmoor (3), on Bodmin Moor (9), and on Dartmoor (12); the remainder (7) are in west Cornwall. The majority thus are in districts away from the megalithic tombs and like the stone rows, may be regarded as the religious monuments of Beaker and Food-Vessel people.

The circles are mostly 70ft to 80ft in diameter with stones 4ft to 6ft high as at Tregaseal, St Just (Plate 6a). Some, like the Merry Maidens, Rosmodress or Brisworthy in the Plym valley, are true circles with the stones regularly spaced: these must have been set out by a thong from a centre point and the stone holes dug at opposite ends of diagonal inter-sections. Others are egg-shaped or regularly flattened circles as at the Nine Maidens, Boscawen-un, the construction of which implies an understanding of simple geometry and the use of more than one centre in setting out. At Boscawen-un and at the Hurlers there is a single up-right within the circle, but not at the centre point. The situation chosen is usually on an open stretch of moorland where ceremonials within the circle would have been visible for some distance; the Scorhill circle on Dartmoor, for instance, can be seen from the rows on Shovel Down (Plate 6b) about a mile away.

Professor A. Thom has interpreted such free-standing circles as a means of calculating and measuring the passing of time based on marking by stones and sightings the rising and setting points of the sun and moon at the solstices, and of stars of the first magnitude. Whatever their purpose, sanctity accumulated at these monuments and led to their multiplication. The Grey Wethers, impressively situated on the watershed between the Teign and the East Dart at 1,400ft, consists of a pair of true circles 30ft apart, whilst at the Hurlers, on the south-east flank of Bodmin Moor, there are three circles in a line, two true circles and one egg-shaped. The same phenomenon may be noted on Mendip at the four Priddy Rings, which are embanked, and at Stanton Drew, where there are three large stone circles and an alignment that leads to the River Chew, Excavation has thrown little light on the people who built the circles or what they did there. At Fernworthy, Dartmoor, the whole of the interior was found to be covered with charcoal, presumably scattered during a ceremony. At the Hurlers it was discovered that the north and the centre circle were linked by a 6ft pavé of granite, and that the interior of the north circle was also roughly paved, but there were no finds. The embanked Stripple Stones, a true circle in the middle of Bodmin Moor, was excavated by St George Gray in 1907 but nothing was found.

In the absence of dating evidence, we have to fall back on the finds from monuments grouped with the circles, which have already been shown to be Beaker at Fernworthy (p 74) and which in west Cornwall are Early and Middle Bronze Age barrows as at the Merry Maidens, Rosmodress or Boskednan, Gulval. Recent excavations at the Druids' Circle, Penmaenmawr, in north Wales by W. E. Griffiths, have shown that this 80ft circle set in a low stony bank was the work of the Food-Vessel people; two children aged ten to thirteen, probably sacrifices, had been buried there after cremation and with each was a plain food-vessel of southern type. It seems likely that some circles in the south-west will prove to be of similar origin. On Dartmoor, their number and widespread distribution indicates prolonged use; some were probably not constructed until the Middle Bronze Age.

We perceive in burial and ceremonial sites a difference in religious practice between the megalithic people and the Beaker and Food-Vessel folk. The sanctity of the circle, essentially an open-air monument, has replaced the dark ancestral tomb; within a circle, whether of stakes, stone uprights or cairn-ring, the dead were buried as individuals and honoured by processions or ceremonial visits along a stone-lined path thereafter. Where did these new ideas come from? Probably from southern England, for the best analogy to the monuments lies in the paired stone circles within the great circle at Avebury, or with the double stone setting of the last phase of the Sanctuary on Overton Hill, both linked by the West Kennet Avenue and, farther west, with Stanton Drew on the Mendips where stone circles and rows are again combined. Excavation has shown that the Avebury monuments stem from a native late Neolithic source, but that it was the Beaker folk who were responsible for the Avenue and for the final form of the sanctuary; a similar derivation is likely in the south-west.

It has often been suggested that Brittany was the source of the western circles and alignments, but only one pair of circles exists there on the island of Er Lannic in the Gulf of Morbihan, now partly submerged. The many impressive alignments on the Breton mainland are on a far larger scale than anything in south-west England, some using more than 1,000 stones, arranged in ten or more lines and terminating in a semicircular enclosure as at Carnac. They are never associated with burial mounds—indeed, they override a Passage Grave and a long barrow at Manio—and whilst their ceremonial use is not in question, the rites were not connected with an interment.

MENHIRS

Finally, the standing stones, or menhirs, which were set up in isolation as well as in the sanctuaries must be considered. These are found throughout the region wherever suitable stone is available, on Exmoor and Dartmoor and are particularly numerous in Cornwall. Many are 10–15ft high and their transport and erection shows great skill. The tallest was Maen Pearn, Constantine, 24ft high, but it was broken up in the eighteenth

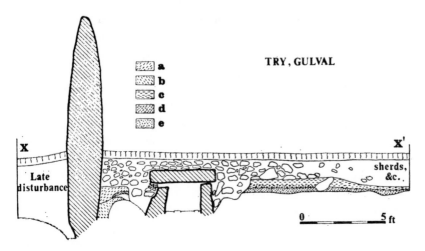

Fig 19 Menhir and Beaker burial at Try, Gulval. Key: a—*medium-brown soft soil;* b—*dark-brown soft soil;* c—*grey leached gritty soil, darker at base of layer;* d—*chocolate-brown weathered rab (?);* e—*rab upcast*

century. The stones have been carefully selected but do not appear to have been dressed; excavation has shown that they were slid into a prepared stone hole and trigged up by a packing of small stones.

In the Land's End peninsula, several were associated with burials. At Try in Gulval parish (Fig 19 and Plate 5b), a handled beaker was buried in a small cist three feet away from the base of a tall menhir, together with some unburnt and some cremated human fragments and covered with a cairn. At Tresvennack, Paul, a large handled Middle Bronze Age urn containing a cremation was deposited in a pit two feet away from the $11\frac{1}{2}$ft tall menhir and a small lugged pot placed a little farther off. Deposits of cremated bones and charred wood are also recorded at the base of three others, at Trelew, Tregiffian, and Pridden in St Buryan parish and also at Trenuggo in Sancreed. At Kerrow, Zennor, a rather different practice was observed; two pots of Middle or Late Bronze Age type were placed one inside the other, on a heap of charcoal, and buried under a layer of stones at the foot of the menhir: they probably contained offerings of food or drink since no bones were found.

79

The two tall stones known as the Pipers near the Merry Maidens circle, Rosmodress, however had nothing beside them, nor had a menhir on St Breock's Down investigated in 1959: such stones may have been cult objects, like the stones on Easter Island.

Excavations at the Long Stone, near St Austell, showed that the present granite monolith, 10ft 3ins high, was the third such monument on the site. It had replaced an earlier standing stone set in a cobbled pavement and overlying a pit containing nine white pebbles; previously the site was marked by a timber post, bedded in the sub-soil. The evidence, slight though it is, indicates that the custom of erecting standing stones started in Beaker times in the south-west and continued well into the Middle Bronze Age, that is from about 1600 till 1000 BC.

The foregoing chapters have made it clear that although we know so little about their domestic life, there was much variety in the peoples inhabiting the south-western peninsula. About 1600–1500 BC, an enterprising trader on his travels by sea-ways and ridgeways might encounter some groups of Western Neolithic stock erecting a chamber-tomb in Penwith, others inserting yet one more cremation burial into an Entrance Grave, or Beaker tribesmen bringing their dead chief for interment in a small cist with his possessions. Other communities as at Tregulland had different funeral rites, involving the setting out of stake circles, and the cutting of protective symbols on the cairn stones. At the sanctuaries on Dartmoor, he might see ceremonies in stone circles or at the raising of a long stone, as well as processions up and down the alignments to the little stone-ringed cairns covering the graves. Both inhumation and cremation were practised. Stone remained the normal material for tools and weapons; only a few of the Beaker chieftains had been able to acquire a small copper or bronze blade. Polished stone axes and the new holed battle-axe continued to be made from the local greenstones, but their export to Wessex was coming to an end.

We have now to see how a more uniform society developed in the ensuing Bronze Age.

CHAPTER V

Prospectors and Traders of the Early Bronze Age

The quickening of life in the south-west in the middle of the second millennium BC, with its resultant changes in settlement and burial customs which we shall examine in this and the next chapter, was due to a stimulus from overseas which affected the whole of southern Britain. Actual immigrants were apparently few, the main object being the opening-up of new sources of metal, and trade in raw materials and in finished goods. In Wessex, in particular, a rich civilisation developed, manifest in the numerous and varied possessions buried with the dead— bronze daggers, flat axes, amber and faience beads, gold ornaments, bronze pins—showing contacts with the metalliferous regions of central Europe on the one hand, and with Eire on the other, and through inter-mediaries, with the Mycenaean civilisation of the Mediterranean. A similar development occurred in Brittany at the same time, shown in the Armorican dagger graves. It might be expected that the south-west, with its rich supply of alluvial tin and with some accessible copper (p. 21), would have shared in this florescence, but whilst some outstand-ing exotic objects were brought here at the outset and in the course of trade, the Early Bronze Age civilisation that developed pales in com-parison with that farther east. This is probably because the land was relatively thinly populated by the Neolithic and Beaker races, and the inhabitants were exploited by the metal merchants.

INHUMATION BURIALS

In Wessex two phases can be distinguished, the first from c 1600–1550 BC being marked by extended inhumation burials under round barrows with triangular copper or bronze daggers with six rivets, the second, starting 1550–1500 BC by predominantly cremation burials with ogival grooved daggers. The early phase is scarcely represented in the south-west, although a find in one of the richest of the Wessex chieftain's graves, Bush Barrow near Stonehenge, shows that contacts existed. This is the perforated stone macehead which is a pebble of Devonian limestone from the Teignmouth district: together with the remarkable bone-mounted wand or sceptre which has affinities in the Mycenaean shaft-graves (and to which the macehead was formerly held to belong) it was probably part of royal insignia.

One outstanding chieftain's burial is in the early Wessex manner, the extended skeleton in a long stone cist in the Rillaton barrow, Linkinhorne, in east Cornwall (Fig 23). The burial place overlooks the rich mineral deposits of Caradon, south-east of Bodmin Moor, and is acessible by ridgeway from St Germans estuary, a western branch of Plymouth Sound. The position of the cist high up in the side of the 120-foot round mound of turf and stone shows that the burial must be a secondary: the grave-goods indicate that he may well be a direct descendant of a prospector. With the corpse was a corrugated gold cup, an ogival dagger and some 'pieces of ivory (bone?), glass (faience?) beads and pottery', now lost.

The fine gold cup (Plate 7a), $3\frac{1}{4}$ inches high, is unique: the horizontal ribbing, and the ribbon-like handle, margined with chased lines and secured by three rivets and diamond-shaped washers, are features that link it with products of Aegean metalworkers. It resembles in technique a pair of small ribbed gold cups from shaft-grave IV, one of the royal tombs in the grace-circle at Mycenae, dating from the sixteenth century BC. The profile at first glance is reminiscent of a Bell beaker but in reality it is a softened version of a biconical form which we shall meet again in shale at Farway (Plate 7b), or in the gold cup from Fritzdorf, Bonn, which in turn was inspired by Mycenaean shaft-grave models.

The Rillaton cup was probably an heirloom when it was placed in the grave with the ogival dagger, and the glass or faience beads in the late fifteenth century BC.

At East Putford in North Devon, an extended inhumation, totally decayed, and with traces of a corroded bronze blade and a wooden pole beside it was buried in a rectangular timber mortuary house, beneath a ditched round barrow of turf. The structure measured 6ft by 4ft between the angle posts and was thought by the excavator, C. A. R. Radford, to be gabled and 3ft high; the top was covered by stones and burnt clay. This too could be the interment of an early Bronze Age chieftain.

There are other massive cists in the peninsula which are large enough to have held an extended inhumation, such as those on Dartmoor at Merrivale and Roundy Park or in Longridge Wood, Roadwater, in Somerset, but there is no record of their contents. At Botrea Hill, Sancreed, although no bones were found, two fine ovate barbed and tanged arrowheads were recovered like those found in the early series of Breton dagger graves, whilst on the cliffs at Trevelgue a handsome boat-shaped stone battle-axe, resembling others found in some early Wessex graves, was associated with a contracted skeleton in a large cist.

CREMATION CEMETERIES

After 1500 BC, contemporary with the second phase in Wessex, the picture is fuller and better defined: we have, on the one hand, a widespread distribution of cremation burials with ogival daggers, necklaces and small cups of pottery or shale and, in Cornwall, with ribbon-handled urns, and on the other the introduction of the conspicuously-sited large round barrow or cairn, some of unusual form, and often massed in an extensive cemetery. Information about settlement and domestic life, however, is still lacking.

The changes are best seen in the Farway necropolis on the Greensand in east Devon, where some 50–60 barrows are concentrated on a narrow ridge that divides the head of the rivers Sid and Coly at a focal point in the hill system and traffic ways (Fig 23). Re-examination of the accounts left by the nineteenth-century antiquaries, R.Kirwan and P.O. Hutchin-son, show that the burials began with cremations by Food-Vessel (Plate 5c) and belated Beaker folk in a small flint cairn. The next stage was the erection of large turf mounds, 80–140ft in diameter, 6–12ft high, some ditched, some surrounded by a free-standing stone circle (Fig 20); these covered cremations which were placed either on a pavement or in a cist beneath a primary flint cairn. The grave-goods were of types new to the area: a grooved dagger, Kimmeridge shale cups and pottery, and

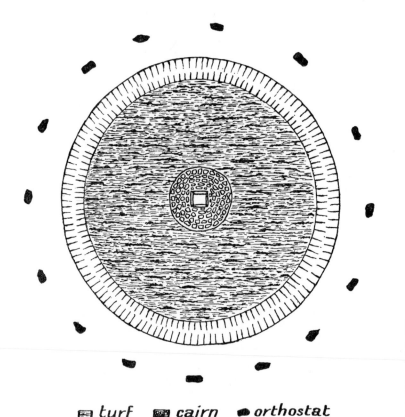

▧ *turf*   ▦ *cairn*   ● *orthostat*

Fig 20 Barrow with stone circle surround and ditch, Farway, east Devon

a segmented bone bead, a form resembling those of faience (p 97) but perforated transversely so that it could be used as a toggle.

The cups (Plate 7b) are fine examples of Early Bronze Age craftsmanship, carved out of soft dark shales from the Kimmeridge beds in south Dorset or from the very similar lignites of the Bovey beds in south Devon. The bases are rounded and it is likely that they were finished by turning on a pole lathe against a flint blade; if so, this is the earliest known instance of turning in Britain. The form is copied from a metal prototype ultimately of Aegean origin and well exemplified in the Fritz-dorf gold cup, whilst the decoration on the handle of the best example is the same as on the Rillaton gold cup (Plate 7a). Similar cups in shale and translucent Baltic amber are among the princely appurtenances in rich Wessex graves as at Clandon, Dorset, with a sceptre, and at Hove, Sussex, with a stone battle-axe. At Farway, both cups were found close to the cremation and so may have been used to pour a final libation. The pottery pygmy cup on the other hand contained the burnt bones of an infant: the two perforations are 'eyes', *oculi*, the protective symbol of the megalithic mother-goddess, well known from the Folkton chalk idols (or 'drums') from Yorkshire.

The new aristocratic element in society is evident also from the arrangement of some of the barrows at Farway: seven of them were set in a row on the edge of the plateau, suggesting that this part of the cemetery was reserved for successive burials of a dynasty. The central mound, which contained a dagger and a shale cup, was the largest; it was probably the first chieftain's burial place. The blending of old and new in burial custom and hence, it can be inferred, in population is shown by the small stone circles of Beaker origin which surrounded two of the mounds (Fig 20). Finally, it can be perceived that these people brought their dead to the cemetery from a wide area and over a long period of time, for the Greensand plateau, uniformly suitable for settlement, is destitute of barrows for many miles around.

Another cemetery of thirty-five large mounds is in the lower Exe valley situated on a patch of well-drained alluvial soils on either side of the river, near Upton Pyne. Typical early grave-goods were found in

1869 in a barrow on Stevenstone farm: a small grooved dagger, a pottery cup and a necklace, wrapped up with cremated bones in a skin or cloth and fastened with a bronze pin (Plate 7c). The eyed pygmy cup was decorated with twisted cord, and the tiny oblate lignite beads and an encrinite (the fossilised stem of a plant) were probably chosen for the necklace because they resembled the shape of segmented faience beads (Plate 8a).

Excavations in 1967 by the Devon Archaeological Society in another barrow in the cemetery revealed a very different state of affairs, of ritual offerings in pots associated with infant burials. At the centre a pot with lug handles containing burnt infant bones and charcoal had been inverted on the old ground surface and then covered with a heap of sand: nine feet away a collared urn of early type was placed in a small sunk stone cist and two other urns of south-western type, with lugs and twisted cord decoration, were put beside it on the ground. Close by in a small scoop, there was a deposit of charcoal on which burnt bones of an infant had been laid. There was nothing in any of the three pots except charcoal and a black substance, probably decayed grass or herbs. All the pots must be contemporary, because they were quickly covered by the barrow, which consisted of three distinct layers, a core of sand, a heap of turves and a final covering of the local red Permian soil. Other instances of ritual barrows are discussed on p 127.

A cemetery of ten barrows near Pelynt, south Cornwall also belongs to this early Bronze Age phase; the barrows, which were excavated in 1830–45, contained cremations, one with an ogival dagger, another with a greenstone macehead, and with a third was the famous short sword or dagger of late Mycenaean type (Plate 10c). As Professor Gordon Childe pointed out in 1951, this square-shouldered weapon with a flanged hilt plate must have been made in the Aegean, perhaps as early as the fourteenth or thirteenth century BC, though the closest analogies are the short swords from a tomb at Diakata, Kephallenia, which have been dated to the twelfth century. The Pelynt find is of great importance because it substantiates the recognition of another Mycenaean dagger— an earlier type resembling those in the sixteenth-century shaft-grave VI at Mycenae—which is carved on one of the sarsen uprights at Stone-henge.

Other cemeteries with early grave-goods in Devon are Huntshaw Cross, Torrington, with a large ogival dagger, and Halwill where an amber pendant of Wessex type was recorded. The occasional bell and disc barrows in some cemeteries as on the Taphouse ridge above the River Fowey (Plate 9) and among the Five Barrows (actually nine) on Exmoor, are also significant, for these forms, in which the burial place is isolated by a berm and surrounded by a ditch and an external bank, are peculiar to early Bronze Age burials in Wessex.

It is already apparent that there was no uniformity in the deposition of the dead nor in the barrow construction in the cemeteries, and the same is true of isolated burials. At North Molton, north Devon, a cremation with a necklace of imported blue faience beads (Plate 8a) and other grave-goods (lost) was simply placed in a cist under a small mound. At Hameldon, 1700ft up on the eastern flank of Dartmoor, the cremation with a grooved dagger having an amber pommel decorated with gold pins *(pointillé)* (Plate 10a) was deposited under a slab pavement but not in the centre of the mound. This was occupied by a small cairn, covering a primary ritual deposit, and the whole enclosed by a cairn-ring, and finally concealed by a mound of peaty turf 40 feet in diameter (Fig 21). Two other barrows further north on the same ridge, Single Barrow and Broad Barrow, are known to be similarly constructed and presumably were erected for the same dynasty.

The Hameldon dagger pommel is a remarkable piece (Fig 22); the form and cruciform decoration show it to be a copy of a well-known Early Bronze Age weapon in southern and central Europe; its pointillé technique can be matched on bone or wooden hilts of daggers in Wessex and Brittany. To reproduce it in amber was a technical *tour de force*, involving the drilling of hundreds of tiny close-set holes for the insertion of gold wire, which was then cut off flush; moreover, the pommel was broken and a repair attempted by rabbeting on the piece and securing the edges of the join with seven more wire pins widely spaced (Plate 10a). Like the Farway shale cups, it indicates that there were craftsmen of a

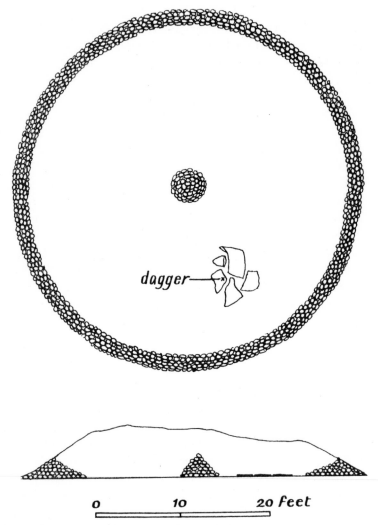

dagger

0   10   20 feet

Fig 21 Plan and section of the Hameldon barrow, Dartmoor

9 Bronze Age barrow cemetery on the Taphouse ridge, Braddock, Cornwall

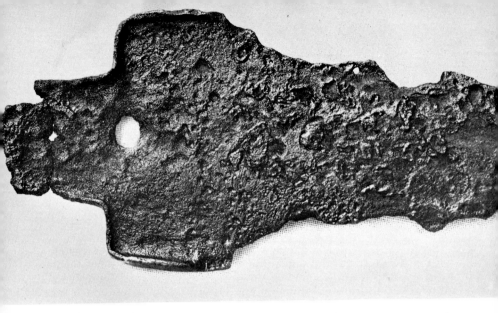

10a (*above left*) Amber and gold pommel of an early Bronze Age dagger from Hameldon, Manaton, Dartmoor. 2·3in by 1·3in. Destroyed 1943

10b (*below left*) Copper shaft-hole axe, imported type, from Mount Howe, Topsham, Devon. Length 4·7 in. British Museum

10c (*right*) Bronze short sword, imported type, from Pelynt, South Cornwall. Length 4·3 in. Truro Museum

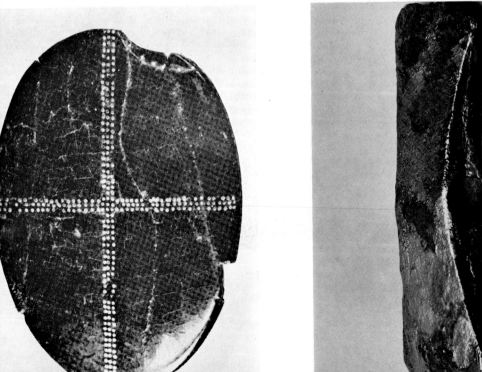

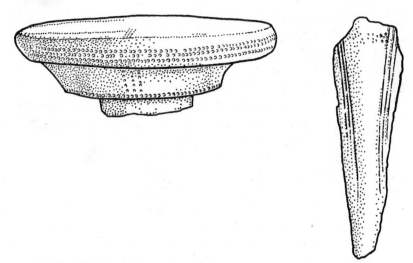

Fig 22 The Hameldon dagger, an amber pommel decorated with gold pins and a bronze blade. Width of pommel 2¼in, length of blade 4in

very high order in the area capable of effecting such a repair for what was presumably originally an imported Wessex piece. It suggests, as does the Rillaton cup, that some of the early prospectors bringing splendid gifts explored the estuaries along the southern coast, and succeeded in establishing themselves in the metalliferous districts of the hinterland.

RIBBON-HANDLED URN-BURIALS

In Cornwall, cremation burials with ogival daggers and other grave-goods are in another mode, in which the bones were collected and placed in a large ribbon-handled urn. These handsome vessels are biconical, tall, wide-mouthed and tapering to a small base (Plate 11a): they are named from the pair of broad loop handles which are applied to the widest part of the urn and through which thongs could be passed for lifting or tilting the pot. The manufacture from the local clays and subsequent firing of these large vessels on an open hearth represent a considerable technical achievement. They are heavily ornamented with impressed cord patterns on both sides of the bevelled rim, and on the neck and handles. The decoration is carefully done, giving an impression either of a plait of three strands, rather like an ear of wheat or a classical laurel wreath, or else of a firm double twist. A typical burial is that in a barrow at Blood Hound Cove, within the sheltered Harlyn Bay on the Cornish coast: with the 20in high urn was a grooved dagger, a little whetstone for sharpening it and an eyed pygmy cup like that from Stevenstone, Devon. Another male burial with a small worn dagger was found at Rosecliston, near Newquay, with the ribbon-handled urn inverted over the cremated bones in a pit in the centre of the 50ft ditched barrow. At Crig-a-Mennis, Perranzabuloe, a magnificent urn—one of two found in the recently excavated barrow (p 127)—contained a plain pygmy cup and some clay beads (Plate 11a). In all, four surviving urns have been found with grooved daggers, five with other grave-goods including faience beads at Carn Creis, and there are thirteen unaccompanied urns, such as that from a cist at Tregaseal, St Just, which was contemporary with an Entrance Grave. Since fragments have been found in Middle Bronze Age settlements at Trevisker, and Gwithian (layer 7) and in the Ash Hole cave at Brixham, the urns had a domestic use, probably as grain storage jars.

The distribution (Fig 23) affects both north and south Cornish coasts; there is no marked concentration in Penwith where the megalithic peoples must have remained strongly entrenched; only later in the Middle Bronze Age when the form and decoration of the urns were modified (Group 2 on p 99, Patchett's Class C) did their makers dominate Land's End. In Devon the early form of the urn is rare; a good example comes from Berrynarbor, near Ilfracombe, lavishly decorated with twisted cord impressions. Outliers in Wessex are of interest as they indicate contacts from 1400 BC onwards: the earliest is the Winterslow urn with plaited cord decoration which was a secondary burial in a Bell-barrow above a primary Bell-beaker interment. With the urn were a tanged razor (Class I), amber beads, and a pygmy cup. Handled urns from Hengistbury Head, Lord's Down, Dewlish, and other places in south Dorset indicate that some Cornish folk also settled west of the Stour in the Middle Bronze Age. This small-scale movement had important effects on the development of later Bronze Age ceramics in Wessex, including the globular urn.

The source of these distinctive and novel pots must now be considered. It used to be thought that they were intrusive and of Breton origin, analogous to the handled biconical pots found in the second series of the Armorican dagger graves. The differences are that the handles of the Breton pots are placed below the rim, not on the girth, they are normally four, not two, and the ornament, when it occurs, is grooved or incised, not corded. Because of these differences, Mr A. ApSimon suggested that prototypes are to be sought in the globular corded amphorae of late Neolithic times in Saxo-Thuringia, which have lug handles on the girth. He sees the Cornish urns as products of immigrants of east German descent coming from the Rhineland and responsible also for the introduction of ogival daggers and for trade contacts with Wessex. It must, however, be admitted that the continental pots

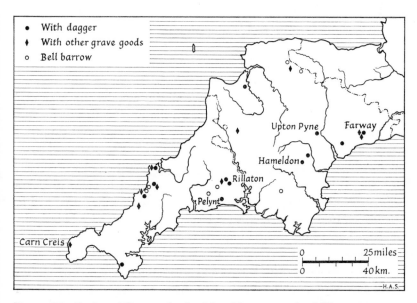

Fig 23 Distribution of Bronze Age burials with grave goods of Wessex type

are not like the Cornish urns in shape, nor in their scheme of decoration, and that they were produced 200 or 300 years earlier. In favour of native development it can be urged that biconical pots, some with lugs, were used by the megalithic peoples, as at Knackyboy or Zennor, that decorated handles were made by Beaker folk at Try (Plate 5b), and that the Food-Vessel people at Farway were acquainted with twisted cord ornament. The decorated ribbon-handles of the exotic Rillaton and Farway cups (Plates 7a, b), could also be related to these urns. At the present state of knowledge no final conclusion can be reached.

Broadly speaking, it is evident that the south-western peninsula formed a cultural province in the early Bronze Age analogous to, and contemporary with, the second phase of the Wessex culture of southern Britain. Within the area, there were regional differences; the peoples in east Devon, and the Exe valley were related to those in Dorset and Wiltshire, whilst those farther west and in north Devon developed different pottery and burial rites. It can hardly be a coincidence that the megalithic colonisation was limited to those western areas and as we have seen, some Penwith and Scillonian tombs were still being used at this time.

TRADE AND METALWORK, IRISH

The lure of metals, of copper and above all tin, was the attraction that brought the prospectors and traders down the English Channel across the Irish Sea, or up the Atlantic coast. Eire had an abundant supply of copper and gold in the Wicklow and Kerry hills, but once it was known that the addition of 10 per cent of tin improved the cutting edge of copper, converting it into bronze, her merchant-smiths had to come to Cornwall and Devon for their supplies (Fig 24). The gifts they proffered in exchange for the black cassiterite pebbles were flat axes and gold insignia, *(lunulae)*. One of the earliest imports is a long thin axe with a characteristic square butt, from Drewsteignton in the Teign valley; later came the round-heeled axes with flanges and crescentic blades decorated with incised geometric patterns found at St. Erth, St Blazey and Sidmouth.

The *lunulae* (Plate 8b) are crescents of gold beaten from a rod ingot

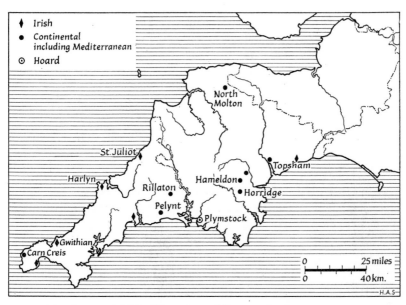

Fig 24 Distribution of Irish and continental Bronze Age imports

extremely thin, to the consistency of stiffened linen, and worn as bibs, or less likely, collars. Their symmetrical decoration of finely chased geometric patterns is derived, according to Dr Joan Taylor, from Beakers in the British insular styles of about 1700 BC. It must not be forgotten, however, that similar motifs were used earlier in Irish passage-grave art on the Boyne, nor that Beaker colonies were established at New Grange by about 2000 BC. In Cornwall a pair of *lunulae* were found with a plain flat axe on the coast near Harlyn in 1865 (Plate 8b), another in a bog on Cargurra farm, Hennet, St Juliot, and a third in 1783 near Gwithian, all within reach of sheltered sandy beaches and the tin streams. The Harlyn Bay find is of particular interest as not only is it the only occasion when *lunulae* have been found with a bronze imple-ment, but one of the *lunulae* has identical decoration to the one in a smith's hoard at Kerivoa, near Guingamp, Côtes du Nord, which was buried in a box with unfinished examples. A third specimen from St

Potan, Dinard, is similar and was probably made by the same craftsman. We can thus identify an itinerant smith plying his trade between Ireland, Cornwall and Brittany.

The evidence for tin working at this time is a dagger (lost) from a tin stream at St Ewe, and what can be deduced from exports. There is the remarkable little necklace from Odoorne found in the peat in the province of Drenthe, north Holland, which has 25 beads of tin strung with 4 of segmented faience, and 14 of amber. Farther east in Denmark there are the handled wooden bowls from burials in oak coffins of the early Bronze Age at Guldhoj, Jutland: these resemble the amber cup from Hove in shape but are decorated *en pointillé* with rows of tin nails round the body and a cross on the base. Their position near the amber coasts and in a region where Irish exports—decorated axes and halberds— have been found must indicate that the Irish merchant-smiths were the intermediaries in the overseas tin trade.

The peoples in Wessex also needed tin and copper for the manufacture of ogival daggers and the newer types of flanged axes: a segmented bead of tin from Sutton Veney, Wilts (lost) shows that the Cornish metal was being exported in the fourteenth century. It is clear from analysis that some copper, with a characteristic high nickel content, was obtained by Wessex from the continent: at present copper of south-western origin cannot be distinguished from Irish metal since both have a high arsenical impurity, and so its exploitation remains uncertain. The large bronze hoard found under a stone at Orston Point, Plymstock, on the estuary of the Plym in 1869 (Fig 24) must represent the stock-in-trade of a merchant-smith, who came from Wessex at this time. It consisted of 16 flanged axes, 3 ogival daggers, a tanged spearhead and a punch or chisel, of which recent analysis has shown that they have a high nickel content. Such finished goods could be exchanged for tin obtainable in the upper reaches of the river on Dartmoor.

MEDITERRANEAN TRADE

We have already seen that in the sixteenth and fifteenth centuries BC, imports of Mycenaean inspiration reached the south-west, which had filtered through from central European sources (p 82). During the fourteenth century the traders brought segmented blue faience beads, manufactured in the eastern Mediterranean (Plate 8a). These appear in tombs of the XVIIIth dynasty at Abydos in Egypt and at Lachish in Palestine, dating between 1450 and 1370 BC as well as in late Mycenaean tombs at Thapsos in Sicily and on Lipari. The distribution indicates that there were two routes from the Mediterranean; a central European route by the Danube to the centres of the Unetice culture in Moravia, and thence by the Rhine to the North Sea, and a western route across southern France by the Garonne to the Atlantic and thence by sea to Brittany. The beads found at Carn Creis in Penwith, and North Molton, Devon, presumably reached the peninsula by the western route, since the bicone beads on the North Molton necklace (Plate 8a) can be matched at Kerstrobel, Finistere, in Britanny. On the south coast a lost necklace from Moor Barton in the Teign valley, south Devon, may have come by the central European route with the consignments of beads to Wessex. It is probable that the art of faience manufacture, using high-grade silica sands and copper as a colourant glaze, was acquired by some communities and that other forms of beads such as the star and quoit shapes which are peculiar to northern and western Britain were made here. A star bead found in the Knackyboy entrance grave in the Scillies (p 59) together with some unique annular blue glass beads are likely to be local products.

Sporadic Mediterranean imports occur on the south coast at a later date. As well as the sub-Mycenaean dagger from Pelynt (Plate 10c, p 86) there is a double-axe of 94 per cent copper from Mount Howe, Topsham, on the Exe estuary (Plate 10b). This with its characteristic oval shaft-hole was undoubtedly made in the Aegean: its closest analogies are in hoards on the Acropolis at Athens and in the late Poros wall area at Mycenae, both dating c 1250 BC. The imports of bronze pins and other objects from the Unetice people which occur in some of the later graves in Wessex and also at Camerton, south of Bath, in Somerset, do not appear in the south-western peninsula: it may well be that during the thirteenth century overseas contacts were solely by the Atlantic route.

CHAPTER VI

South-Western Bronze Age Societies

There is no doubt that the centuries from 1500–1300 BC were the formative period in Bronze Age culture and society throughout the south-west. It was, as we have seen, a period of stimulus from overseas trading contacts, from which followed the welding together of the mixed late Neolithic, Beaker and Food Vessel stocks under new leaders, some being immigrants in the first place, others appearing no doubt in response to the challenge of the times. This epoch was succeeded by a long period of relative stability, from 1300–450 BC, or even later in some districts, when there was no radical change in the population or in their way of life. During this period there was a steady increase in the population shown by the number and size of the settlements with their associated fields and stock enclosures and by the multiplication and spread of barrow burials, until in certain areas like Dartmoor the habitable land must have been fully taken up.

CHRONOLOGY

The difficulty of this long period, until very recently, has been its lack of fixed points to which to attach a chronology. Weapons and ornaments, which are dateable, now ceased to be placed in the graves and owing to the acid soil have not survived in the settlements on the granite. The excavations of numerous huts which took place in the late nineteenth and early twentieth centuries were unskilfully conducted and inadequately recorded; consequently no sequence of stratified pottery was established and the whole issue bedevilled by the wishful thinking of the local antiquaries who had proclaimed that everything was 'Early Bronze Age' or 'Neolithic'. Nor were the domestic wares, mostly found in Devon, correlated with funerary urns, mostly found in Cornwall: apparent differences were emphasised and likenesses overlooked so that the essential cultural unity of the peninsula remained unappreciated.

Excavations in the post-war period have changed this situation. In Cornwall, sherds of ribbon-handled urns have been found in huts at Trevisker, St Eval, enabling Mr A. ApSimon to work out a sequence of pottery styles starting in the early Middle Bronze Age, and to correlate it with the development of the funeral urns. At Gwithian, an open settlement on dunes by the Hayle estuary, Professor Charles Thomas has obtained a stratified sequence with three layers of Bronze Age occupation separated by blown sand. The last of these (layer 3) was dated by two bronze pins with south German affinities to the period 1300–1100 BC and by a mould of local stone for an early form of socketed axe, the north-east German type which occurs in the Bishopland and Taunton hoards, and which is dated *c* 1000–900 BC. From Dartmoor, pottery has been obtained from an enclosed settlement on Dean Moor, Avon valley, which can be placed in the Cornish sequence, whilst at Kestor, Chagford, an iron smelting furnace in a hut showed that the culture survived till at least 600 BC.

Pottery

Pottery is now the key to a new chronology. It falls into three stylistic groups, developing one from the other at Trevisker, and successively stratified at Gwithian.

The early group is characterised by cord ornament, principally the laureate plait: it includes the biconical ribbon-handled pots (Plate 11a) previously described (p 91) and dates from the second Wessex phase, *c* 1500 BC (Trevisker style 1; Gwithian layers 7–8; with Beaker sherds).

In the middle group, cord ornament continues but twisted impressions now predominate. There is much incised or grooved decoration done with a rounded point and some prodding: 'dimple' impressions, cruci-form 'ribs' of applied clay on the base, and flat cordons on the body now appear (Plate 11b); loop and lug handles continue. The large pots are either rounded or straight-sided; most rims have an internal bevel, although some are everted. (Trevisker styles 2 and 3; Gwithian layer 5 with radio-carbon date of 1120 BC.)

In the late group, cord ornament has died out, incised patterns continue, either narrow scratched lines at Gwithian, or untidy broad ones on Dartmoor (Plates 11b c). Square lugs and flat cordons continue on straight-sided and globular pots; rims are flat-topped, tapering to a thin body, or have an internal bevel (Trevisker style 4; Gwithian layer 3, dated 1200–900 BC).

In Cornwall the later wares are harder and better fired: in Devon there is no change until the introduction of early Iron Age ceramic with everted rims, carination and fingertip ornament as at Kestor, Foales Arrishes and Dainton.

SETTLEMENTS

The study of pottery styles, however, is only a means to an end; it enables us to arrange settlements and burials chronologically so that the stages by which man came to terms with his environment can be ascertained. Broadly speaking, there are two ways of getting a living from the land, by arable cultivation and by stock-keeping: both were practised by the Bronze Age peoples, not exclusively but in varying proportion by different groups. It is these differences in economy, not in chronology, that define the settlement types.

Pastoral

First the pastoralists: these lived in enclosed and/or nucleated settlements surviving principally on Dartmoor and Bodmin Moor. The walls of the enclosures are substantial, built with a facing of granite boulders and a core of small stones, 7–9ft thick and probably 6–8ft high. Inside there are usually five to ten scattered round huts, but sometimes as many as twenty to thirty; single huts are rare. There may also be stock-pens attached to the main wall, as at Rider's Rings in the Avon valley (Fig 25). On Dartmoor these settlements are distributed thickly in the southern

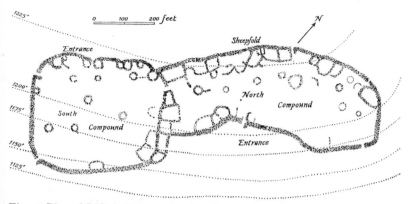

Fig 25 Plan of Rider's Rings enclosed settlement, Dartmoor

and western valleys, on the south-facing slopes between 1,000ft and 1,300ft (Fig 26). Their relation to water and to good grazing is obvious, as on the Erme where settlements occupy successive tracts of moorland divided by tributary streams (Fig 17). The Legis Tor settlements were built at the edge of the River Plym whilst Grimspound, Manaton, which lies in a fold in hills between Hameldon and Hookney Tor, was sited on a small stream, the Grims Lake which flows under the wall (Plate 12a).

Indications that there was cultivation in the enclosure are rare. Soil washes downhill naturally after heavy rain particularly if it has been trampled by cattle, and in piling up behind the wall on the lower side has a deceptive appearance of a lynchet, as at Trowlesworthy. At Rider's Rings there are some sub-rectangular walled plots in the centre of the double enclosure, which look like cultivation patches (Fig 25), and elsewhere the placing of huts only on the perimeter of an enclosure is suggestive. A broken saddle-quern and rubbers at Dean Moor in the Avon valley shows that some grain was grown but the cultivation plots were not located.

There are also open village settlements in which the huts are linked by low walls forming irregular enclosures, that could be used for cultivation or for stock. Some of these settlements are very large, for example sixty-eight huts on Standon Down, and ninety-four at Watern

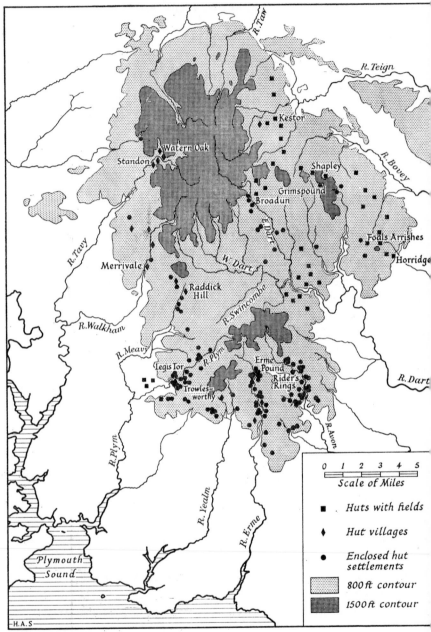

Fig 26 Distribution of Bronze Age settlements on Dartmoor

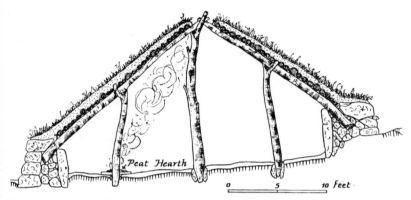

Peat Hearth

0   5   10 feet

Fig 27 Reconstructed section of a Dartmoor hut at Kestor, Chagford, Devon

Oke, both in the upper Tavy valley, and there are similar settlements on Bodmin Moor, as at Rough Tor. Their layout indicates a mixed economy, predominantly pastoral.

The huts are circular, varying from 10–25ft in internal diameter, with walls 4–5ft thick and of the same height. They were entered by a narrow doorway, which faced away from the piercing north-west wind, and sometimes screened by a curved wall forming a sort of vestibule as at Grimspound or by a timber porch at Stannon Down, Bodmin Moor. Excavation at Dean Moor has shown that their conical thatched roof was supported on a central upright post and a ring of six or seven others, 3ft or 4ft away from the hut wall (Fig 27). The principal rafters rested on these and on the wall-top, wedged amongst the large stones, and converged at the apex where they could be secured to the centre post. Lighter timbers would be fastened to the rafters, and the remaining space filled with supple hazel or alder branches, as a foundation for a reed or heather thatch. Looking upwards in the gloom inside the hut, the roof structure would look like a spider's web, with a hole in the centre for the smoke to escape. In the smaller huts in settlements like Grimspound, the roof was constructed wigwam fashion without internal supports. At Heatree Down, Manaton, some of the stone huts were preceded by slighter constructions using many small stakes and wattle work.

103

The large circular hut with an interior post-ring has a long life in this region: it begins at Trevisker and Dean Moor in the Middle Bronze Age and occurs in an irregular oval form at Gwithian (p 67) about 1500 BC. It persists throughout the Iron Age as at Kestor, at Bodrifty and at Castle Dore hill-fort, despite the occasional appearance of rectangular forms at Glastonbury lake village (p 147) and Blackbury hill-fort.

At Dean Moor, the evolution of an interior house plan is perceptible (Fig 28). The lower side of the hut was the kitchen and working-

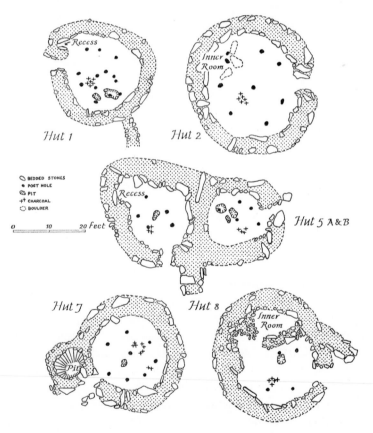

Fig 28 Hut types in the Dean Moor enclosed settlement, Dartmoor

quarters: the hearth was here, edged with small stones and nearby were several small pits or holes, 1–2ft deep, in which food was cooked by covering it with hot ash or with heated river pebbles. At Raddick Hill on the Meavy and at Legis Tor on the Plym, whole pots were found sunk in such holes, presumably to prevent upset, and to keep their contents cool. The upper part of the floor, which was levelled into the hillside, was relatively clean and in two huts was separated by a setting of boulders (Hut 2) or by a low wall (Hut 8) to form an inner room, the sleeping quarters. In hut 5A, one of two huts that can only be called semi-detached, this clean floor extended to form a recess 5ft 3in by 4ft, which may be compared with the 'neuks' for box-beds surviving in some Orkney crofts today. These developments from the primitive open house plan, which has become fashionable again in the mid-twentieth century, show the beginnings of a desire for privacy and imply a change in Bronze Age society away from the communal habitation.

Pottery from the Dartmoor pastoral settlements belongs to the middle and late groups: the pots from Raddick Hill (Plate 11b) and the Dewerstone are representative.

Arable

The arable settlements are open with the dwellings placed in a group on the edges of the fields, or in a yard as at the Rippon Tor homestead on Dartmoor (Fig 29). Two to four huts with six to eight fields make up a small settlement, and represent the holding of a family group. The fields, which are lynchetted, are small, one third to half an acre: they are edged by a row of granite slabs and boulders which have been cleared off before ploughing, and sometimes reinforced by a packing of small stones and soil. At Gwithian, in west Cornwall, there was some evidence that thorny brushwood had been used for a similar purpose. The fields are normally rectilinear and squarish, a shape suitable for cross ploughing, though elongated fields do occur as at Horridge on Dartmoor (Plate 13a) or at Stannon Down on Bodmin Moor.

At Gwithian the actual plough marks have been preserved: they show up either as brown bands of humic soil in a base of yellow sand (Plate

13b) or where the last furrows have been filled by blown sand, as yellow stripes on a brown soil-base. The furrows are 3–4in deep, V-shaped with one side vertical and one oblique, widely spaced from 1ft to 2ft apart and they cross and intersect, showing clearly that the field was ploughed both ways, as advocated by Virgil in the *Georgics* (I: 97). These marks were produced by a light wooden plough, a 'crook ard', made from a bent bough with the tip hardened for the share by charring: such ploughs are depicted drawn by oxen on Bronze Age rock carvings at Monte Bego in the Alpes Maritimes and have been found in peat bogs in Jutland dating from the Iron Age. Places on the edges of the fields where the plough could not reach were dug over with a spade at Gwithian, which left D-shaped marks (Plate 13c) 4–5in deep, similar to those made by a long-handled shovel with a pointed blade such as is used in Cornwall and west Wales today. This and the spacing of the furrows wide enough for a man to walk between, indicates careful husbandry. Barley, both naked and hulled varieties, was grown on the evidence of impressions on Cornish Middle Bronze Age pottery.

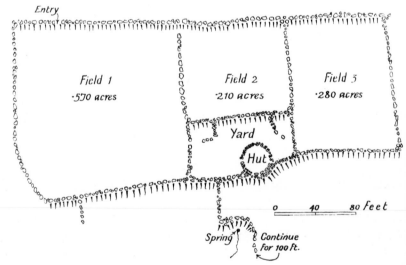

Fig 29 Homestead at Rippon Tor, Ilsington, Devon

11a *(above)* Ribbon-handled Bronze Age urns and miniature cup from Crig-a-Minnis barrow, Perranzabuloe, Cornwall. Heights 14in, 15·5in, 2·5in. Truro Museum 11b *(below left)* Storage pot, from Bronze Age settlement at Raddick Hill, Meavy, Dartmoor. Height 10·5in. Plymouth Museum 11c *(below right)* Urn from a Middle Bronze Age barrow, Elworthy, Somerset. Height 9·25in. Taunton Museum

12a *(above)* Grimspound, enclosed Bronze Age settlement, Manaton, Dartmoor 12b *(below)* Hut and field walls at Kestor, Chagford, Dartmoor

On Dartmoor some family holdings expanded and multiplied until their fields coalesced, and extended over nearly a mile of moorland, as at Kestor, Foales Arrishes or Horridge (Plate 13a). The original field pattern often has been altered by medieval cultivators combining several fields into a long strip. There are droveways between the field-walls to the open moor, showing that grazing was an essential part of the economy.

The distribution of the agriculturalists (Fig 26) is complementary to that of the pastoralists, being concentrated on the eastern side of Dartmoor, with a small overlap only in the valleys of the East Dart and Plym. The explanation is geographical: not only has the eastern side a considerably lower rainfall, but the soil, Brown Earth (Moretonhampstead type), is more fertile and is therefore better suited to cereal cultivation. It follows that the settlement types are, broadly speaking, contemporary and belong to the same people or culture.

The huts in the arable settlements (Plate 12b) are noticeably larger and better constructed than those in the pounds and villages. They measure 20–30ft in internal diameter, exceptionally 30–40ft with walls 4–5ft thick, lined with massive granite slabs. Excavation has shown that the roof of turf or thatch was supported on a centre post and a post-ring (Fig 27) as in the pounds and a division into sleeping and working quarters was also discernible. An unusual structure was the large metal worker's hut at Kestor, walled off from the fields in a circular enclosure known as Round Pound (Figs 30, 31). Its roof was supported on an irregular setting of posts, a single row over the working quarters, with its

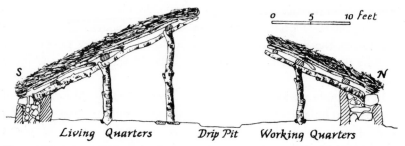

Fig 30 Reconstructed section of the metal worker's hut at Kestor, Chagford, Devon

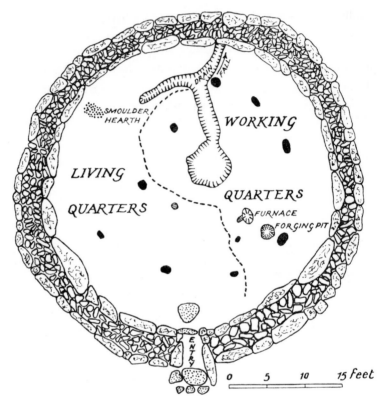

Fig 31 Plan of the metal worker's hut, the Round Pound, Kestor, Chagford, Devon

iron smelting furnace and forging pit, and a double row over the living-sleeping quarters where there was a subsidiary hearth. There was an opening in the roof, eccentrically placed over a shallow pit probably used by the smith for quenching, and a covered drain led from it under the wall.

In the arable settlement on Stannon Down, Bodmin Moor, some of the eighteen huts were divided radially by screens of hurdling, traced by rows of stake holes. Wooden furniture such as a shelf or dresser about 18ins wide was indicated by lines of postholes following the curve of the hut walls, whilst straight settings suggested a bed, a couch, a loom or a table.

The arable settlements are broadly contemporary with the pastoral group, though some earlier and later sites are known. Smallacombe Rocks, a settlement of four huts with at least three fields, has produced furrowed storage jars with elaborate plaited cord decoration that belong to the early group (p 99). The pottery from Stannon is similar to that from Gwithian (layer 5) and has been dated by R. Mercer to 1200–1000 BC. A farmstead in the extensive field system on Horridge Common (Plate 13a) was apparently in being by 1100 BC when a 'Bohemian' palstave, an imported central European type (Fig 33b) was dropped in one of its fields. Some farms were still in existence in the late Bronze Age and early Iron Age, as at Kestor or Foales Arrishes, using carinated and finger-tip ornamented pottery and smelting iron for their implements.

On Bodmin Moor also, a settlement of small huts set amongst fields on Garrow Tor, excavated by Miss D. Dudley, was occupied in the third century BC on the evidence of an imported La Tène I blue and yellow glass eye-bead. It is clear that once farming communities had established themselves in the uplands, their mode of life remained unaltered for a very long time.

Bronze Age settlements were not of course confined to the granite moors where their remains are obvious, but were widespread through-out the region as the distribution of barrows and metalwork indicates: the sites are gradually being located. Pottery from the Ash Hole cave, Brixham, and at Prawle shows there were fishing communities on the south Devon coast. At Tredarvah, Penzance, a metal worker's hut was found with finished goods, slag and domestic pottery, both cord orna-mented and incised: the bronzes (p 117) enable the occupation to be dated to about 1200–1100 BC. The settlement at Gwithian on the dunes near Hayle has already been mentioned (p 105): the farm contemporary with the ploughing has not been located but there are remains of three slightly later huts which impinge on the fields. They were built of turves on a slate and rubble foundation, with the roof supported on an irregular oval setting of posts 3ft to 4ft away from the walls: two of the huts had timber porches. The hearths were circular, edged with beach pebbles and in a clay-lined hollow beside them a saddle quern and rubbing stones were kept. This settlement had a long life, being occupied throughout the Bronze Age, apart from an interval when it was abandoned due to blown sand. There is a radio-carbon date of 1120±100 BC from a hearth (layer 5) contemporary with the field system.

A new type of settlement has recently been found at Norton Fitzwarren in the Vale of Taunton: this is a hill-top enclosure of five acres, defended by a bank and ditch, foreshadowing the fortifications of the Iron Age; a Middle Bronze Age date of about 1100 BC is assured by the concealment of a hoard consisting of a bundle of eight bracelets (Fig 32), two south-western palstaves and an early socketed axe. The inhabitants were using typical south-western Middle Bronze Age pottery with cord and incised decoration.

METALLURGY, TOOLS AND WEAPONS

Many of the settlements on the granite were well-placed for the ex-

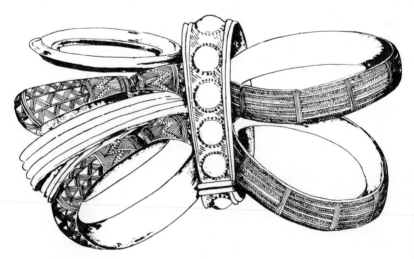

Fig 32 **Bronze bracelets, from Norton Fitzwarren**

ploitation of alluvial tin and of the copper lodes, but evidence that the metals were worked is elusive. A hoard of tin nodules from a Middle Bronze Age hut at Trevisker and a droplet of slag and a cassiterite pebble from huts at Dean Moor, are the only authentic records. It can be deduced that the smelting furnaces were situated in the mining area and not in the settlements. The surprising discovery of 50lb of broken iron ore, a high-grade specular haematite, in the core of a hut wall at Dean Moor shows that the inhabitants prospected five or six miles of the granite for metals. Since the double process of smelting and forging necessary to extract workable iron was not known, the ore was regarded as waste, probably after failure to smelt it.

Middle Bronze Age

It seems reasonable to infer that the local metals were used for the manufacture of regional types of tools and weapons. The most common

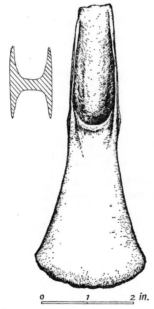

Fig 33a Palstave of south-western type from Bovey Tracey, Devon

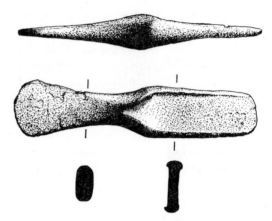

Fig 33b Palstave of continental type from Horridge, Dartmoor

tool was the palstave, an improvement on the early flanged axe by the provision of a stop-ridge between the base of the blade and the hafting hollow, and by the increased height of the flanges to grip the split 'knee' shaft. The south-western form (Fig 33a) is a heavy tool, with a broadly expanding blade, often with a raised Y or V pattern below the stop-ridge, and with characteristic high flanges, which distinguish it from the low-flanged varieties of southern and eastern England. The distribution (Fig 34) shows a concentration in the surrounds of the Somerset marshes and in Devon; a stone mould from Bigbury in the Plymouth Museum shows that the type was made in Devon. A hoard of eight found under a granite boulder at Plumley, Bovey Tracey, in 1836 must represent a metal-worker's stock, whereas the two found with the rapiers at Crediton (Fig 35) should be the personal equipment of a chief.

The rapier too was produced locally; two sets of bi-valve stone moulds were found in the alluvial clay under 6ft of river gravel in the metalliferous Teign valley at Knighton, Hennock (Plate 14b). The moulds had been tied together in pairs, as though ready for casting. On the longer mould a matrix for casting a five-ribbed tapering strip has been cut, suitable for making bracelets and rings, like those in the Edington Burtle ornament hoard in Somerset. The edges of the smaller mould have thin diagonal vents for the escape of gases during casting: this, as Mr H. Hodges has pointed out, was a custom of the bronze-smiths of northern Europe and was not a British or Irish practice: it suggests that the moulds at Knighton came from the workshop of an immigrant travelling smith. A similar mould of greenstone was found at Polcoverack, in the Lizard, suggesting coastal movement of the metal workers.

Ten rapiers are known from south Devon: they include a merchant's hoard of six at Talaton on the ridgeway between the Otter and Clyst, two from Crediton found with the palstaves (Fig 35), and one from Fice's Well, Princetown, which was sealed under 18 inches of peat. Such weapons are a reminder that the Middle Bronze Age was not always peaceful.

There are other signs of contact between the bronze smiths in the south-west and those on the continent in the Middle Bronze Age. There

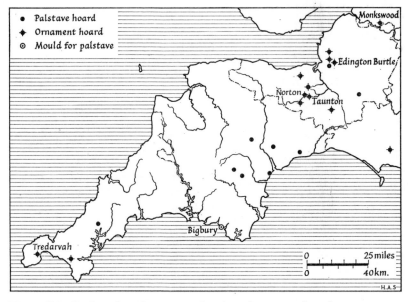

Fig 34 Distribution of south-western palstave and ornament hoards

is the 'Bohemian' palstave found in the Horridge field system (p 109) which differs from the local examples in having low flanges which converge to form a V-shaped stop-ridge (Fig 33b). This probably came from East Germany, where there are metal workers' hoards, for example at Neuhaldensleben on the Elbe, which include this type and also the high-flanged palstave of south-western British origin. Trading contacts with the Netherlands are also indicated by the hoard of six south-western palstaves at Voorhout, Drenthe.

The Somerset ornament hoards reveal links with continental practice. These are a group of hoards in the Vale of Taunton (Fig 34) and on the periphery of the Levels in which the native types of palstave and spear heads are found in association with torcs or necklets of twisted bronze, decorated bracelets, finger-rings, pins as well as knobbed sickles. These, as Dr Margaret Smith has shown, derive from foreign models current in north-east and in southern Germany about 1200–1000 BC (Monteilius III). That these exotic things were made locally is shown by the

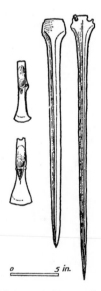

Fig 35 The Crediton hoard of bronze rapiers and palstaves

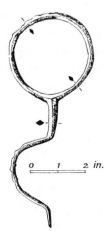

Fig 36 Quoit pin, from the Taunton Workhouse hoard, Somerset

casting faults on the bracelets (Fig 32) as well as the axe in the Norton Fitzwarren hoard (p 112). One of the knobbed sickles in the Edington Burtle hoard, which was found in a maple-wood chest by peat diggers in 1854, was likewise an untrimmed casting straight from the mould. A rare type of slender socketed axe in the Taunton and Norton Fitzwarren hoards which originated in East Germany was copied in the region on the evidence of a stone mould from the Gwithian settlement (layer 3). It affords another chronological and cultural link between the farmers and the smiths.

The local smiths were also inventive and produced large bronze pins with loop heads, known as Quoit pins, which are unknown on the continent. They are found in the Somerset hoards and also in the Tredarvah hoard in a metal-worker's hut near Penzance, associated with a high-flanged palstave, a socketed spear, a tanged knife and a pin with a side-loop.

A West Country connection with Iberia is indicated by the palstaves with two loops, which are found in central Somerset, with outliers at Chagford, Devon, and St Mawgan-in-Meneage, south Cornwall, as well as on the Dorset coast. This double-looped form was manufactured in north-west Spain and Portugal in the late Bronze Age, where moulds and untrimmed specimens are known. In Britain its association with a twisted torc and a bracelet at West Buckland near Taunton, shows that it was contemporary with the 'ornament hoards' like Edington Burtle, assigned to the late Middle Bronze Age.

The ornaments that are such a feature of the Somerset hoards show that a display of jewellery and elaborate dress became fashionable locally in the Middle Bronze Age, as on the continent; for instance, little bronze cones in the Monkswood hoard, near Bath, are thought to be for stitching to a skin-cloak, like one worn by a woman buried at Lübz, in east Germany. It is unfortunate that the adoption of cremation in Britain has prevented us from seeing the Middle Bronze Age chieftains and their women in their finery in the grave. The hoards show that neck-lets, bracelets (Fig 32) and rings were worn and the large quoit pins probably were used to fasten clothing.

The same fashion for adornment is reflected in the contemporary or slightly later Towednack gold hoard (Plate 15), which was found buried in a field bank, presumed to be Bronze Age, not far from St Ives. Here there were two splendid twisted torcs, four plain bracelets, two being unfinished, and three slender coiled bars of gold, the smith's raw material. Both torcs were made from such gold bars by heating and working them into triangular form and then beating out the angles slightly into low flanges, except the terminals which were left plain and rounded; the whole was then tightly twisted clockwise, bent into form and the ends turned back as long hook fasteners. The larger torc, which is 45 inches long and was found in two coils, probably was intended for a spiral bracelet *(armilla)* of four or five coils. The smaller torc, $4\frac{1}{2}$ inches across, is a technical *tour de force*, being made of three separate strands, each regularly twisted and united at the terminals. This hoard must be the stock-in-trade of a travelling Irish smith, exchanging products of his native gold, made to a customer's order, for Cornish tin; it provides a glimpse of the smith in relation to local society, *c* 900 BC.

Late Bronze Age

It is now generally agreed that there was no radical change in the last phase of the Bronze Age in the south-west. The period from 900–450 BC is marked only by the successive introductions of new varieties of bronze tools and weapons, by an increase in the smiths' output and in the exploitation of metals. The rapier gave way to the heavy slashing sword with a leaf-shaped blade and elongated hilt, the palstave was replaced by a variety of socketed axes and a wide range of tools, socketed knives, gouges and chisels, all ultimately of continental origin, became available for the carpenter's and metal-worker's tool-chest. Nevertheless in comparison with southern and eastern Britain, the new elements are few in number and limited in kind; there are only three swords from Devon and six or seven from Cornwall, of which only one survives; in Devon, palstaves outnumber socketed axes by two to one indicating their prolonged use; founder's hoards are few; none of the West Alpine novelties which are regularly associated with carp's tongue swords and winged axes in the south-east or the harness trappings which appear in the latest South Wales hoards are found: in short, the peninsula became rather a backwater.

Three of the founder's hoards reveal the smiths at work. At Kenidjack Castle, St Just, some thirty pieces of copper and smelted tin were found in a hut outside the rampart of the Iron Age promontory fort; with these was a broken winged axe suitable for melting down, and two new socketed axes of south-western type with three ribs, made of bronze with a high tin content. At Wick, Stogursey, on the north Somerset coast, a hoard of 147 pieces was found in 1870. It contained several copper ingots and also bronze 'jets', the surplus metal remaining in the clay funnel when it was poured into the mould. The seventeen pieces of swords, a broken chape, thirty-seven damaged axes and spearheads and a couple of palstaves were material collected for the melting pot, whilst the socketed axes, gouges and knives were new products ready for sale.

A characteristic type of socketed axe was made in the south-west. This is a heavy tool with three converging or divergent ribs and with a broad flat-topped moulding round the socket. Two sets of stone moulds for these came from Helsbury, near Camelford (Plate 14a): they are unusual in having a guide line on the ends for keying the moulds together instead of dowel holes, and in the matrix being cut flush with the top of the mould, instead of providing a hollow for the insertion of the clay core and pouring 'gate'. The distribution of such axes is practically confined to the south-west and to South Wales: since the majority have been found in Glamorgan, it is often called the Welsh axe, though no workshop has been found there. From its association in hoards on both sides of the Bristol Channel, for instance at Kenidjack with a discarded winged axe, and at Llynfawr with cauldrons, harness trappings and an iron Hallstatt sword, it was manufactured towards the end of the Bronze Age, probably in the seventh or sixth century BC.

Another socketed axe mould was found on the Quantocks and is of bronze which was more usually employed than stone at this time. It is said that such bi-valve moulds were used by the smiths for the quick production of bees' wax models for casting by the *cire-perdue* process; but as Mr Hodges has pointed out, the cutting of two recesses at the mouth of the Quantock mould is a device to prevent a clay socket core riding up during casting, so it can be presumed that they were employed for direct casting. No axes from the mould have been found so it is evidently the work of an isolated local smith.

Another type of hoard is the bundle of spears, complete with ferrules, that was deposited in Bloody Pool, a tarn now dry, in the Avon valley, near South Brent. Three of the four surviving were a heavy barbed form, fastened on to the shaft by a stout metal peg below the barbs: such spears are mostly found in the Thames valley and in the Welsh Marches. The type is impractical and was apparently evolved for ceremonial use. We can deduce that this hoard was a votive offering, to the spirit of the pool.

Although the south-west lay outside the main stream of continental connections in the late Bronze Age, trading contacts with Brittany and with Ireland were maintained. From Brittany came characteristic straight-sided square-socketed axes, of which forty or fifty were found at Higher Roseworthy, Gwinear in 1880, and others on Carn Brea, near Redruth. Two were found in a tin stream under 12ft of black mud at Lanherne, St Mawgan-in-Pyder, together with other socketed axes, a saw, a Middle Bronze Age rapier and palstave. These Breton axes are curious in that many of them are non-functional, being badly made of thin metal, often with a high proportion of lead and with the casting seams left on and the blade unsharpened. They are found in great quantities in the Breton hoards and it is probable that they were used as a primitive currency both in their homeland and for export. It is difficult to suggest what brought their merchants to the south-west, since Brittany possesses both tin and copper of her own and they had no need to cross the Channel for it.

The Irish finds are more spectacular: they include a hoard of six gold bracelets from Morvah in the Land's End peninsula, three with attractive hollow trumpet-mouth ends, two with solid expanded terminals and one with folded-back ends: the type with expanded terminals occurs in the well-known Beachy Head hoard with a carp's tongue sword and a winged axe and is of seventh-century date. Two large bronze vessels found in 1792 by tin miners working on Broadwater Moor, Luxulyan, near St Austell, but unfortunately not preserved, are likely to be of Irish manufacture and late Bronze Age date: one was said to be a conical vessel hammered out of a single sheet of bronze, perhaps a bucket, the other was a cauldron made of strips of bronze riveted together and had elaborate attachments for the handles on the rim; similar cauldrons were exported from Ireland in the seventh and sixth centuries to Wales, southern Britain and the Atlantic coasts, so this Cornish find falls into place on a recognised trade route. There are other cauldron fragments in the collection from Mount Batten, Plymouth.

Towards the end of the Bronze Age, the climate deteriorated as the warm wet sub-Atlantic phase set in, accelerating the growth of blanket peat on the high moors and culminating c 500–400 BC in an inundation in the Somerset levels, which became a sedge fen. The onset was gradual from c 900 BC: to overcome it, Late Bronze Age peoples living on the perimeter and the islands and on the Polden ridge built timber trackways and platforms on the surface of the raised bogs. The trackway across Meare Heath which has been traced for $1\frac{1}{2}$ miles, consisted of a corduroy of heavy oak and birch timbers on a brushwood foundation and held in place by stakes driven through square mortise holes: the stakes also retained a kerb of longitudinal timbers, presumably for the benefit of wheeled traffic. Radiocarbon analysis has dated timber in this trackway to c 880 BC ($\pm$ 110), but other tracks on Shapwick Heath belong to the sixth century. They reflect the vain struggle to maintain communications against the rising flood waters.

BARROWS

We turn now to the burial rites of the Bronze Age people as revealed by the numerous barrows raised to their dead. A conservative reckoning based on the Ordnance Survey maps shows about 875 surviving in Cornwall, 550 in Devon. They are found not only on the granite moors but on some of the Culm clay ridges in mid and west Devon, around Halwill, Holsworthy, and in the Hartland peninsula. Their distribution reflects the well-known improvement in the sub-Boreal climate, which permitted the colonisation of heavier soil. The distribution on the moors is apparently unrelated to the settlements: for instance, in the Avon valley, south Dartmoor, there are 33 settlements containing over 200 huts and only 8 barrows on the surrounding hills. Obviously the graves of the majority of the population were not permanently marked and not even that of every chieftain.

Siting

The site chosen was usually a summit from which the mound is conspicuous over a wide tract of country, as for example Three Barrows at 1,550ft above the Erme on Dartmoor, or Chapman barrows at 1,575ft on Exmoor: others were erected at intervals along the ridgeways as on the Brendon Hills whilst on the plateaux and lower ground the barrow is often placed on a 'false crest', and is conspicuous from one approach. The dead were thus set apart from the likely settlement zone, the lower ground by the springheads, but interred in places where they were brought to mind as men and women moved about the hills with the herds.

The grouping of the mounds implies that individual communities had their own burial grounds, well exemplified on Exmoor in the clusters of barrows along the 1,500ft ridge between the Barle and Bray on the present Devon–Somerset boundary. In such cemeteries, the cairns are irregularly spaced as in the Five Barrows (actually eight); only exceptionally are they aligned as the seven out of the eleven in the Chapman group. In other districts, the barrows may be dispersed over more than a mile of plateau as at Halwill, or on the Taphouse ridge east of Lostwithiel, leaving the surrounding area blank.

Construction

The mound was built either of stones, turf or earth, or was a composite consisting of separate deposits of each, as at Chapman Barrow (Fig 37) or Upton Pyne (p 86). The use of turf is common, avoiding the necessity of ditch digging to obtain soil. The sods were used to build steep-sided mounds often with a flat top, from which ceremonies could have been performed: the type is frequent on the ill-drained soils in mid-Devon. Small stones were collected and used to build a cairn-ring: at Hameldon (Fig 21) this marked the edge of the mound; at Chapman Barrow (Fig 37) it encircled a turf stack but was covered by soil, whilst at Crig-a-Minnis (Fig 38) only a segment was built which was covered by the mound. At Elworthy in Somerset a circle of upright stones, which were 3ft high, surrounded a cremation in an urn with boldly incised decoration and was concealed in the body of the mound: similarly at Higher Draynes, St Neot, Bodmin Moor, there were circular

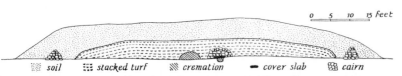

Fig 37 Reconstructed section of a barrow in the Chapman group, Challacombe, north Devon

revetment rings incorporated in the cairn. A revetment of large blocks either laid horizontally (a kerb) or set upright (a peristalith) was frequently built at the circumference of cairns on Dartmoor (the so-called retaining circle), on Exmoor as at Setta Barrow and in Cornwall: they were functional, they retained the sods or stones and enhanced the final appearance: the concealed features, on the other hand, were magical, designed to protect the ashes of the dead from molestation and to confine the spirits to the tomb.

Burial Rites

It is now axiomatic that a barrow is not just a heap of earth or stones covering a burial, but the result of a series of ritual acts and constructions by a community, which it is the task of an excavator to elucidate by slow and careful work. The rough and ready methods of the eighteenth- and nineteenth-century antiquaries and their inadequate records do not provide the material for this sort of interpretation, and since very few scientific excavations have taken place in this region, our knowledge is limited.

Single cremation burials were the normal method of disposal of the dead. The ashes were collected from the pyre and brought to the chosen site and buried, often in an urn, which was sometimes placed in a pit, but more frequently in a small cist below ground level and covered by a flat slab. The place was then usually marked by a small cairn or mound before the full-size barrow was built, as for instance at Chapman Barrows on Exmoor (Fig 37). Such monuments, in effect, are a tribute to the individual, reflecting presumably his or her importance in the community; the concept originated with the Beaker folk and is evident in the inhumations of the early Bronze Age (p 82): on the evidence of the urns, it continued to dominate funeral practice during the Middle Bronze Age.

Secondly, there are multiple interments, as for example, the four cremations in urns, one in a cist, one inverted on a flat slab and another erect, found under a round cairn at Clahar Garden, Mullion. Others described by W. C. Borlase are Carn Creis with five urns, one ribbon-

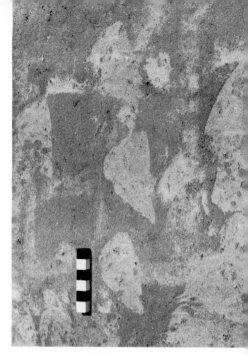

Bronze Age agriculture 13a (*above*) Huts and fields on Horridge Common, Ilsington, Dartmoor 13b (*above right*) Plough marks from the Bronze Age settlement, Gwithian, Hayle, Cornwall 13c (*below right*) Bronze Age spade marks from Gwithian

14a *(above)* Stone moulds for casting bronze socketed axes, from Helsbury, Cornwall. Length 4·7in and 5in. Truro Museum 14b *(below)* Stone moulds for casting bronze rapier, from River Teign, Hennock, Devon. Length 21·5in. Cast, Exeter Museum

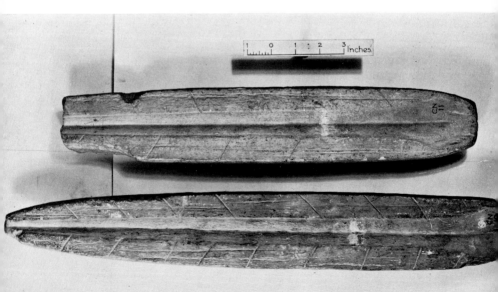

handled and one with faience beads, Carn Leskeys with seven urns and Trannack, Madron, with five or six urns. The surviving urns from these barrows vary in style and form but there is not enough evidence to decide whether such burying places were used for some time as a flat cemetery before being covered by the cairn or barrow, or whether the burials were simultaneous. A flat cemetery with urns in style 1 and 2 has been found at Port Mellon, Mevagissey. In these interments the mega-lithic idea of communal burial is in evidence and it is not surprising that all known examples are in Cornwall. The Entrance Graves (p 59) which contain a succession of cremations, some like Knackyboy in similar Middle Bronze Age urns, are another expression of the same idea.

Thirdly there are ritual barrows, in which the primary deposit consists of charcoal or other substances in a central pit or beneath a small cairn. The human remains, whether one or several, are buried usually in urns some distance away, in a manner aptly termed by Ashbee as 'satellite burial'. The implication is that a ritual act, which probably was believed to establish contact with the underworld, preceded the burial and was of prime importance; the classic example is Sixwells in Glamorgan excavated in 1940 by Cyril Fox. In our region the Hameldon dagger burial previously described (Fig 21, p 87) is a dated instance of a satellite to a small cairn covering only charcoal. At Brownstone Farm, Kingswear, an early Bronze Age cremation with a miniature polished jadeite axe in a stone cist was placed 8 feet away from the centre of the mound at which there was a small hole tight-packed with the burnt bones of a child of ten; the primary ritual act implied here is a sacrifice. There is also a growing number of barrows where despite proper excavation, no burials are recorded. Combe Beacon, a large turf barrow 10ft high with a central cairn of chert at Combe St Nicholas in Somerset, covered only a small hole domed over with loamy soil and filled with oak, ash and hazel charcoal. At Crig-a-Minnis, Perranzabuloe (Fig 38) the low central cairn concealed only a deposit of oak charcoal spread on the old ground surface and filling a small hole; two fine ribbon-handled urns (style 1) and a miniature cup were buried in little pits 15ft to 20ft away in different directions (Plate 11a): neither urn contained human

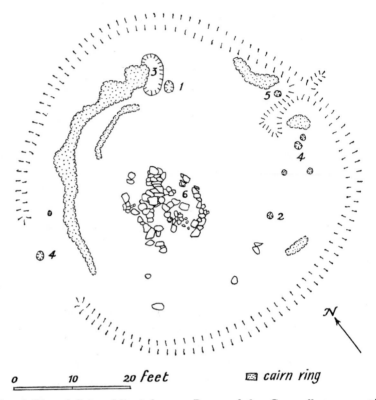

Fig 38 Plan of Crig-a-Minnis barrow, Perranzabuloe, Cornwall. 1–2, urn pits; 3–4, ritual pits; 5, miniature cup; 6, stone area

remains and two other pits contained only charcoal. The area was partly enclosed by a cairn-ring and a ditch with a ramped entrance. before being covered by a turf barrow with a capping of white quartz. It would have been a striking monument in the landscape, and though the excavator, Mrs Christie, concluded it was a cenotaph, it is more likely that it was, like Upton Pyne (p 86), a sacred place for offerings. Excavation of barrows at Stenalees, St Austell in 1972 by Mrs Miles, revealed a similar sanctuary. One proved to be a circular embanked enclosure in which a circle of posts had been erected round a granite boulder and two small pits had been dug behind it. Their contents had been disturbed but scattered around them were white quartz pebbles, a bit of amber and of a remarkable bone (?) copy of a Wessex dagger with pointillé decoration of the blade. An adjoining turf mound, 8oft in diameter with a kerb of stones, had only a small upright stone in the centre: there was an entrance through the kerb indicating a way up to the flat top of the mound.

It must be concluded that many Bronze Age communities had such a sacred place where ritual acts and ceremonies were performed and offerings made; we only know of them when they happen to have been covered over by a mound or enclosed, as on Burnt Common by a cairn-ring (p 68).

Two conclusions emerge from the records of barrows opened in this region: first, there was no uniformity in burial practice or barrow construction, even in one district, or among examples that have produced the same sort of pottery. Each community must have built up its own tradition, new elements perhaps being acquired through marriage. Secondly, whilst Bronze Age funeral practice embodies several elements with a Beaker or Megalithic ancestry, the elaboration of barrow building is associated with the earlier forms of ribbon-handled urns (style 1) or with Wessex grave-goods, on present dating to c 1400 BC. Apparently no new rites or structural innovations were introduced after the beginning of the Middle Bronze Age and whilst barrow building still continued to be extensively practised, the traditions were in decay. There are very few barrows containing pottery that can be assigned to the late Bronze Age with any certainty at present, though there are many on record which contained plain cremations which may belong to this epoch. On the other hand, it is probable that before 900 BC the custom of barrow-making had died out in the south-west and that people were buried in flat cemeteries or in other ways which as yet have eluded the archaeologist.

CHAPTER VII

The Celtic Peoples

During the Iron Age immigration began again from the continent; groups of Celtic peoples crossed from northern and western France and Belgium to settle in strength in southern Britain. They came in three waves, the first in the seventh and sixth centuries BC with pottery and equipment of late Urnfield and Hallstatt types that had been developed on the continent during the previous 200 years; their culture is known as Iron A, and is poorly represented in the south-west. The second wave, the B groups, brought a fully developed La Tène I culture, characterised by decorated metalwork and pottery; they effected first local infiltrations, which were followed by a massive and widespread intrusion in the south-west in the fourth and third centuries BC. The last wave, the C groups, came to Britain from the late second till the mid first centuries BC in consequence of the invasions of Gaul by Germanic tribes, the Cimbri and Teutons, in 120–110 BC and by Julius Caesar in 58–50 BC: the Belgic tribes of south-eastern and southern England were the principal intruders but other small refugee groups can be distinguished in the south-west. At the end of the Iron Age, an amalgam of these Celtic peoples in the peninsula, together with Bronze Age survivors on the high moorland, were known as the Dumnonii, and were so named by the Greek geographer, Ptolemy, when he compiled his map at Alexandria in the second century AD.

Celtic society differed in many respects from the preceding Bronze Age civilisation. The population was politically more unified and organised in larger units, in tribes under chieftains and in tribal confederacies under kings. Women also played an important part in the social order judging by the rich possessions buried in their graves. The struggles between the tribes for land and wealth made the Celts an alert, adventurous and bellicose people. Warfare now was a major pre-occupation, shown both in the labour diverted to building elaborate fortifications and in the craftsmanship devoted to the panoply of the warrior-chiefs. Under the aegis of the Dumnonii the trade in Cornish tin flourished, with Gallic merchants acting as middle-men for the Mediterranean market; Diodorus Siculus records that they found the inhabitants peaceable and friendly to strangers. Agriculture however was the mainstay of the economy and as we shall see in the hill-forts, stock-keeping rather than corn-growing was predominant.

THE FIRST PHASE

Settlements and Burials

It is difficult to be certain whether there was any significant change in the population at the beginning of the Iron Age because the first Celtic peoples differed little in their way of life from the Bronze Age agricul-turalists (p 100). They too lived peasant-fashion in open settlements in round huts and cultivated small fields as at Bodrifty on the granite near Penzance or at Dainton on the Devonian limestone near Newton Abbot. The main difference lies in the pottery they used, which includes charac-teristic small bowls and tall-necked pots with a carination and splayed rim common to the early Iron peoples in southern Britain. At Dainton a ferruginous slip was used to redden the surface of some vessels in imitation of the haematite wares of Wessex, whilst at Bodrifty some fine wares were burnished. Some Bronze Age sherds at Bodrifty are evi-dence for continuity of population whilst on Dartmoor the few Iron Age sherds from huts at Kestor and Foales Arrishes show that some newcomers were absorbed by the native population in the upland.

They brought, however, to this region the knowledge of iron working which had eluded the metalworkers at Dean Moor (p 113). The process differs from that of tin and copper smelting in that the metal has to be extracted from the ore in two stages: the first smelt produces only a spongy bloom that is full of impurities; it has then to be reheated, hammered on an anvil and quenched to purify, toughen and consolidate the metal. In the metalworker's hut at Kestor (Figs 30, 31) the dual process was in evidence; there was a small bowl furnace full of iron slag, the residue from the last smelt, a forging-pit burnt red, a quenching place with a drain and an anvil stone. The ore used was a specular haematite from the Hennock district ten miles away. The new metal thus produced was malleable; tools and weapons no longer had to be cast and were easier to produce and to repair. Communities were no longer dependent on the itinerant merchant-smith for their everyday needs, which was a real advance.

The Celtic peoples re-introduced inhumation burial: at the large cemetery found beneath 15ft of sand-dune in 1900–05 at Harlyn Bay, Padstow, the dead were buried in a contracted position in rectangular coffins of thin slate slabs. Grave-goods included a bronze swan-neck pin and two iron-ring headed pins; also two La Tène I brooches of a type found in north-west Spain, earrings and a bracelet, which date from the late fourth and third century BC. The same rite of cist burial with the corpse contracted and adorned for burial persisted throughout the Iron Age and into the Roman period. It can be seen for instance, in another grave at Trevone near Padstow where a woman was buried wearing a shale armlet and a pair of unusual La Tène I brooches, one of iron with a glass inlay and one of bronze of the British involuted type, both dating to c 200 BC. In later cemeteries at Mount Batten, Plymouth and Trelan Bahow, St Keverne, noble women wearing bracelets, beads and La Tène III brooches were interred with their decorated mirrors (Plate 20) or with imported glass vessels early in the first century AD and at Porth Cressa and Poynter's Garden in the Scilly Islands in the first and second centuries AD. At Harlyn Bay there was a midden beside the cemetery, indicating there was a settlement at this sheltered site. The occupants made needles, awls and borers for leather from the local slate as well as loomweights and spindle whorls for their weaving and spinning. They also used bone weaving-combs and bobbins whilst a quantity of *Purpurea lapillus* shells, from which purple dyes are extracted, shows that they may have produced coloured cloth. The brooches of an Iberian pattern in the cemetery suggest that there were visiting traders to the bay, if not immigrants, from the Atlantic coasts in the fourth or third centuries BC. Decorated pottery from the midden shows that the occupation continued into the second and first centuries BC.

At Mount Batten, the promontory on the eastern side of Plymouth Sound, an important trading settlement was established, taking advantage of the sheltered anchorage and of easy routes to western Dartmoor and to the metalliferous regions south-east of Bodmin Moor. Bronzes and pottery from a midden on the shore show that the site was occupied from the Late Bronze Age and throughout the Iron Age, starting with bucket-shaped situlate jars of southern type with which a swan-neck pin and another example of an Iberian La Tène I brooch can be associated. There were also several ribbed and knobbed bronze bracelets of late Hallstatt or early La Tène continental patterns, for which the nearest source would be Normandy or Brittany, and which indicate cross-channel trading contacts.

Re-examination of the structures and finds from Glastonbury lake village (p 147) suggests that the original settlement was effected early in the Iron Age and may well be contemporary with these sites.

Fortifications

In the south-west as yet there is no evidence of an initial phase of sophisticated hill-fort building with timber-laced ramparts similar to those recently discovered at Crickley Hill, near Gloucester, and dated to the seventh and sixth centuries, or even earlier, according to the radio-carbon evidence from some forts in the Welsh Marches. So far as can be judged, the beginnings of fortification generally began in the fourth century BC, perhaps in response to a threat of further invasions. Blackbury Castle started about this time as a single ramparted fort of four acres on the narrow back of a greensand spur in east Devon. The plain pottery used has affinities with that produced by late Southern Iron A people at Maiden Castle, Dorset. The gateway to the fort was strongly fortified by building up the out-turned ends of the rampart with layers of chert, clay and flint nodules which were held in place by a timber palisade: in effect the door was flanked by low semi-circular towers or fighting platforms which were connected by a timber bridge set back over the gate. In the interior the only dwelling found was a rectilinear timber house with an oven and cooking pit. Later an unusual barbican outwork was added, though it remained unfinished: it probably functioned as stockpens on either side of an embanked approach road. At Woodbury Castle, near Exmouth, recent excavations have shown that the hill-fort was preceded by a hutted settlement enclosed by a palisade: the plain pottery, found beneath the later ramparts, is probably contemporary with that from Blackbury.

At Maen Castle, on the wind-swept granite cliffs above Sennen Cove, Land's End, a small promontory was fortified by another early group, using plain undecorated pottery. The defences were a thick wall of granite blocks packed in soil, with a berm separating it from the ditch, and a counter-scarp bank. There was a single entrance, facing east towards a zone of small terraced fields. Since no permanent dwellings were found in the fort, the builders presumably lived in a more sheltered spot beyond the cultivation.

It is only because these forts have been carefully excavated that we are able to assign them to an early phase of Iron Age settlement: there are many univallate forts and cliff castles such as Cadson Bury near Callington or Golden at Probus, that may prove to have originated at this time, or earlier in the light of radio-carbon dates elsewhere.

Overseas Trade

It is apparent that from the sixth century BC there were trading contacts between south-west Britain and the Armorican peninsula. The late Latin poem *Ora Maritima* of Avienus incorporates fragments of a very early topographical account of the north-western coasts, known as the Massiliote Periplus, by a Greek voyager. From this, it is learnt that Tartessians from southern Spain and Carthaginians voyaged as far as Brittany *(Oestrymnis)* and its offshore islands to trade: thence the natives sailed in skin boats to Ireland which is called Ierne and to Britain which is called Albion.

Early in the fifth century the Carthaginians conquered Tartessos and gained control of the rich mineral deposits in southern Spain which had supplied the Greek city states in the Mediterranean; thus a fresh demand arose for tin from north-west Europe. This is the economic background to the voyage of Pytheas, a Greek merchant and geographer, who in 330–325 BC sailed up the Atlantic coasts to Britain and the far north. His account unfortunately has not survived except in quotation by later writers; his experiences, for instance, are referred to by Strabo in his *Geography* but only usually to disparage them. By the second century BC it is clear from the *History* of Diodorus Siculus that regular trade routes from the Mediterranean to Britain were established, a thirty days march overland from the Rhône to the Garonne via the Carcassone gap, thence by sea to Corbilo (Nantes) on the Loire, and on in fair weather to round the Armorican peninsula and a four days' voyage 'across Ocean' to south-west Britain. Gallic merchants were the intermediaries, principally the Veneti from southern Brittany until the savage destruction of their fleet by Caesar in 56 BC.

Archaeological confirmation of direct contact with the Mediterranean is slender and frequently suspect, but continues to accumulate. There are a pair of two-handled Attic cups *(borsae)* and a jug *(oinochoe)* in the Torquay Museum from 'an artificial cave at Teignmouth' which can be assigned to the fourth century BC. At Holne above the Dart near Buckfast a worn silver coin of Alexander the Great and another of Aesillas the Roman quaestor in Macedonia in 90 BC were found separately by a ploughman and seem genuine imports. In Exeter, apart from a mixed collection of Mediterranean coins found in Broadgate in 1810–20 which remain suspect, copper coins of the cities of Velia and Paestum in south Italy were found in 1931, though unstratified; others were recorded by a reliable antiquary, Captain W. P. Shortt in the 1830s and 1840s. Recently a hoard of forty-three silver drachmae has been recovered from Paul, near Penzance, minted by Celtic tribes in Cisalpine Gaul and modelled on those of Massilia: their date lies in the late second century BC.

There is thus a growing body of evidence that cannot be disregarded. Not all these tokens were necessarily exchanged for tin. Diodorus also states that in Gaul merchants would give a jar of wine for a slave (V. 26). The great H-shaped tin ingot weighing 158lb and 'shaped like an *astragalus*' as Diodorus described it (Plate 17b), which was dredged up near St Mawes, Falmouth, must be but one of many that were brought down by packhorses or wagons to be loaded into the ships of the Veneti, anchored in the deep estuary or off St Michael's Mount *(Ictis)*.

THE SECOND PHASE

The effective Celtic settlement of the peninsula took place in the late fourth and third centuries BC by peoples from north-western France who had been in contact with the advanced La Tène civilisations of the Marne; they introduced new varieties of pottery and metal work and developed a regional style of fortification suited to a pastoral economy. Their culture is termed South-Western Third B in Professor Hawkes' classification: the movements of earlier groups (First B) to the south and east of England, and the resulting fusion with the A peoples there (Second B cultures) are not really represented in the south-west which pursued an independent course.

Pottery

The new decorated ceramic, which is the hall-mark of South-Western B is a dark smooth ware which has been burnished or sometimes worked over with wet hands to produce the appearance of a slip: the bowls and jars are rounded with a well-marked neck and everted rim, sometimes finished on a turn-table or slow wheel. The decoration is boldly incised as a band on the shoulder, using a 'blunt point'. The patterns which resemble those on metal-work (Plates 16a,b,c) are of scrolls and curves, often emphasised by surface moulding, particularly by a depression at the head of a scroll, whilst other elements are brought out by an infilling of diagonal or cross-hatching: in the best examples there is a subtle inter-play between the plain and hatched

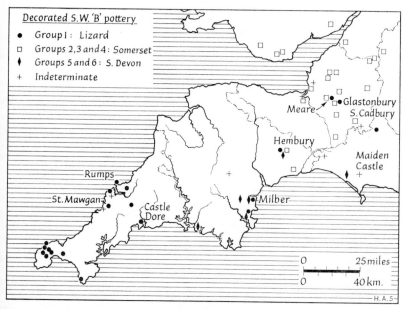

Fig 39 Distribution of decorated pottery of the south-western Third B type

surfaces. An internal groove on the lip of both plain and decorated pots is also a characteristic innovation.

Recent petrological work by David Peacock has identified the constituents of the clays and tempering and has indicated that these decorated wares were produced only at few centres, presumably by specialist potters, and distributed widely (Fig 39). In Cornwall the gabbroitic clays of the Lizard peninsula were used (Peacock Group 1) as they had been in Neolithic times (p 37). These pots were decorated with simple curvilinear patterns, broadly tooled as on examples from Castle Dore or St Mawgan (Plate 16c): they were distributed throughout Cornwall and occasionally exported to Devon, Dorset and Somerset. Another type of decoration is a row of S- or Z-shaped impressions, made with a wooden stamp, which are the vestiges of a row of stylised ducks. Such stamping is an earlier fashion that is found sporadically in Brittany and more frequently in north-west Spain and Portugal. In Britain similar wares were produced by Iron Age potters in the Malvern region and distributed generally in the lower Severn and Welsh Marches. It is uncertain whether the few Cornish examples made of the gabbroitic clay are local copies of continental or British examples.

Other centres of pottery manufacture were in north-east Somerset utilising clays derived from the Mendip and Jurassic limestones and from the Old Red Sandstone, probably of Beacon Hill, Shepton Mallet (Peacock, Groups 2–4). These wares are more sophisticated than the Cornish: the potters used a fine point for the tooling and had a larger repertoire of designs, including motifs like the swastika, fret, triquetra and returning spiral. The wares are distributed mainly in north Somerset, much of it at the lake villages of Glastonbury and Meare, where it was first discovered by Bulleid and Gray and named 'Glastonbury ware'. A third centre was established in south Devon as is evident from the inclusions derived from the Permian formations (Peacock Groups 5–6): the pots have simple geometric decoration, as at Milber Down hill-fort (p 142) and were distributed locally for the most part (Fig 39).

The origin of the decorated pottery and the people who made it is still obscure though Brittany remains the most likely source. In general, Breton La Tène pottery of the third and second centuries is different but there are a few pieces like the decorated jars from St-Pol-de-Lèon and Plouhinec which have long been held to be ancestral to the British series. These have incised designs with a stippled infilling, which are transcripts of those on Marnian metalwork of the fourth century BC; some simple patterns like the scallop or broken arcading occur in Cornwall, Somerset and in the Morbihan. The pots with internal-grooved rims are also a type which is localised in north-western France and south-western England as Sir Mortimer Wheeler has shown. However it is clear that decorated pottery was popular in south-west Britain, and in company with the metal-work, regional styles developed which are not found on the continent.

Hill-Forts

The numerous settlements of the 'B' people were nearly all fortified:

they vary in size, scale and layout from that appropriate to a small homestead to that of a large tribal *oppidum*. They are built not only on sites with good natural defences, but also on hill-slopes and on plateau sites. Their builders did not, however, penetrate beyond the fringes of Dartmoor and Bodmin Moor, leaving the upland to the Bronze Age hut-dwellers (Fig 40).

Very few hill-forts have been excavated and their classification and interpretation is based mainly on surface inspection. We can distinguish three categories (i) Large forts with single or multiple close-set ramparts, (ii) Forts with several enclosures, formed by wide-spaced

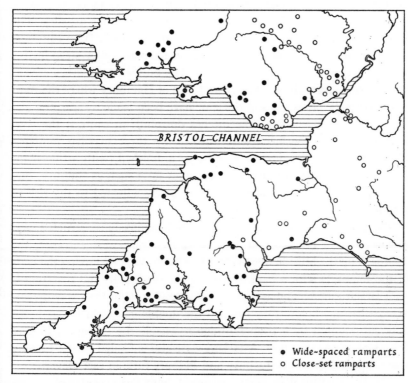

Fig 40 Distribution of multivallate hill-forts excluding cliff-castles

ramparts, (iii) Small forts with single ramparts, promontory forts and cliff-castles being included in these groups.

(i) These large forts *(oppida)* are all defensively sited, occupying the crest of hills or the end of a spur, as Dumpdon and Hembury forts near Honiton or a seaward promontory as at Trevelgue (Plates 18a, b). The size ranges between 3 and 15 acres; among the largest are Carnyke where a single earth rampart and ditch is aligned along the contour of an isolated hill near Bodmin, and Countisbury near Lynmouth where the top of a steep spur between the sea and East Lyn river is defended by a massive bank and ditch across the neck. In the multivallate forts, the inner rampart dominated the defences: the succession of close-set ditches and outer banks were built as obstacles to be crossed when the attackers came into range of sling-stones and other missiles. The ramparts usually were of *glacis* construction, the upcast from the ditch being formed into a continuous slope so as to create a long steep incline which gave no foothold for an assault. The builders took every advantage of the natural slopes: this is well seen at Hembury where the ramparts along the steep sides of the spur have been made by scarping and by throwing the soil from the ditches downhill: in contrast the level approach across the neck was fortified by three massive ramparts thrown up from the ditches, one being unfinished, with artificial inclines that measure 50–55ft long. In other forts such as Sidbury, east Devon, the size of the ramparts is also nicely adjusted to the risk of attack.

The entrances in this class of fort were ingeniously constructed, and obviously were the focus of attack. At Hembury west entrance, the approach up the hillside was made into a bottle-neck by linking the ends of the ramparts with a bank screening the ditch ends and revetting it with large timbers. The assailants would have to fight their way up this narrow passage before they reached the double gate, which was probably surmounted by a timber bridge to enable the defenders to pass from one side to the other. Attackers were also enfiladed by out-turning the rampart ends as at Musbury and Sidbury forts in east Devon.

The large multivallate forts are found, with few exceptions, to east of the Exe (Fig 40). Their designs are closely linked with the forts of the Durotriges, the tribes in Dorset and south Somerset. Nevertheless Hembury was built by peoples using south-western decorated pottery, whom we may now call the Dumnonii.

The multivallate cliff-castles on the north coast of Cornwall must be the work of another overseas group entering the Bristol Channel. The great fort on Trevelgue Head, Newquay (Plate 18a), with four close-set ramparts defending the narrowest part of the promontory, an inner enclosure and an outer annexe is obviously a work of several periods but since the excavations of 1939 are unpublished, its origin remains an enigma. Similar massing of ramparts can be seen in promontory forts in south Wales as at Castle Ditches, Llantwit Major, and is also a feature of the first fort at Worlebury, Weston-super-Mare, which has four lines of defence across a limestone spur. The triple rampart fort on Gurnard's Head is structurally related to a Breton fort, Kercaradec, near Quimper: excavation has shown that both have a massive inner stone rampart, with a vertical face and stepped back, providing a stance for slingers. The same feature has been found at two promontory forts in County Cork, Portadoona and Carrigillihy, which suggests a colonising movement by Veneti up the western seaways in the third century BC.

It should be added that there are a few large forts on the granite that have dry-stone ramparts, like Trencrom, a fine contour fort near St Ives or the Cheesewring on Bodmin Moor, at which rocky outcrops were skilfully incorporated in the circuit. The Dewerstone promontory fort on the western fringe of Dartmoor was defended by two dry-walls, whilst Chun, Land's End (p 193) has a massive inner wall and an outer rampart. It is not yet clear whether this use of stone is of cultural significance, indicating some fresh immigrants, widely dispersed but with a common building tradition, or more likely whether it is due to using what was easiest and customary on the granite.

(ii) The multiple-enclosure forts are numerous and widespread west of the Exe and on Exmoor; they have good claims to be a regional type, although they are also found in South Wales and occasionally in southern England. Some of them are defensively sited, like Prestonbury in the

Teign gorge (Plate 19b) but many are hidden away on hill-slopes, and on wooded spurs overlooked by higher ground and so at a tactical disadvantage if attacked. These forts consist of a circular or sub-rectangular inner enclosure of $\frac{1}{2}$ to 4 acres, with one or more larger outer enclosures, either concentric with it as is Clovelly Dykes (Plate 19a) or dependent from it as at Castle Dore, or annexed to it as at Helsbury. A favourite site is the end of a spur where the outer enclosure could be defended by a crossbank as at Hall Rings, Pelynt (Fig 41). Some cliff-castles also have wide-spaced ramparts, for instance Embury Beacon in the Hartland peninsula.

The ramparts are small-scale, and in contrast to the multivallate *oppida*, the outermost is usually the largest, as at the concentric fort Tregear Rounds, St Kew. The entrances are simple; sometimes the rampart ends were knobbed or thickened as at Clovelly, rarely inturned as at Prestonbury or screened as at Pencarrow. The line of approach through the enclosures was sometimes embanked as at Wooston or Resugga and often deeply worn, indicating the regular passage of stock. Frequently the entrances are orientated towards springs and the outer ramparts are aligned to control them, showing the importance of a water-supply.

The layout of these forts provided a defended dwelling place for a chieftain and his kin in the innermost enclosure, with accommodation for stock in the outer enclosures, secure against cattle raiders. At Clovelly Dykes (Plate 19a) there are four zones of outworks with restricted entry, suggesting segregation of the herds for milking, or for autumn slaughter.

Excavation at Castle Dore and Milber has shown that the inhabitants were using decorated B pottery from the beginning: imported La Tène glass bracelets and beads at Castle Dore show that this fort was in being by 250 BC, whilst Milber near Newton Abbot, was built before 100 BC and went out of use before AD 25. Several forts have surface signs of enlargement or re-fortification, which indicate a long life. Analogies for the fort plans can be found in some of the *castros* of Galicia and Orense in north-west Spain but their peculiarities can also be explained as in-

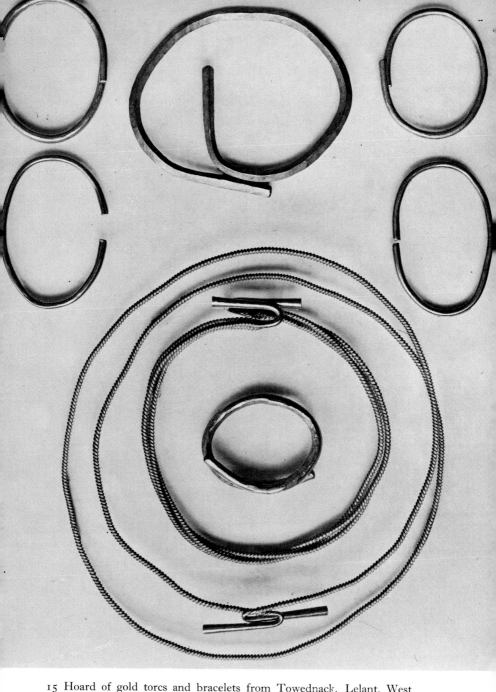

15 Hoard of gold torcs and bracelets from Towednack, Lelant, West
Cornwall. British Museum

Iron Age pottery, south-western types. 16a, b *(above right, left)* Meare lake village, Somerset. Height 4·7in, 13·7in. Taunton Museum 16c *(below left)* Carloggas hill-fort, St Mawgan-in-Pyder, Cornwall. Height 7in. Truro Museum 16d *(below right)* Hembury hill-fort, East Devon. Height 3·7in. Exeter Museum

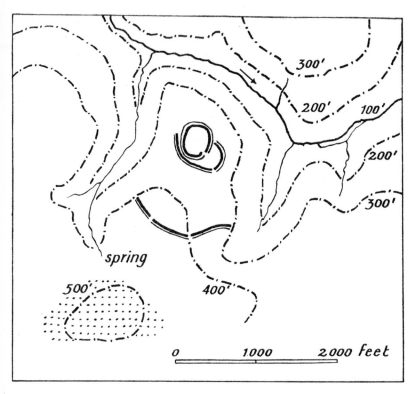

Fig 41 Plan of Hall Rings hill-slope fort, Pelynt, Cornwall

sular developments, due to the adoption of a pastoral economy suited
to the south-western environment.

Rounds

Small forts defended by a single rampart are known as Rounds in
Cornwall: they are numerous in mid and north-east Cornwall, and also
occur in mid and north-west Devon. They are generally situated on
undulating ground between 200ft and 400ft and in Cornwall on land
that is good for arable cultivation. Most of them are circular or oval
enclosures of half to two acres with a simple entrance by a causeway

I   145

across the ditch; a few are rectilinear like Trevinnick, St Kew, which excavation has shown to be of early Roman date.

Excavation at Castle Gotha, St Austell, has shown that the defences of this one and a half acre oval enclosure were erected before 100 BC and that the occupation continued well into the second century AD. The inhabitants lived in timber huts built in the lee of the ramparts; they included metalworkers who used clay-lined pits, hearths and a stone mould for casting pennanular bracelets. An ingot mould was also found embedded in the latest floor in one hut, probably for tin from the nearby Pentewan streams. At Trevisker Round, St Eval, only two large huts were built in the oval two-acre enclosure, which superseded the Bronze Age open settlement (p 99). Iron Age pottery used at both sites included plain and decorated south-western B wares.

The Rounds are thus more like a defended hamlet or homestead built by a kin-group rather than a hill-fort built by a tribe; in scale and character they are not unlike the enclosed Bronze Age settlements on the granite moors (p 100). In Ireland the type is known as a rath or ring-fort, and had a long life, continuing through the Dark Ages and early Christian period, and it would not be surprising if some Cornish examples were inhabited also in post-Roman times.

Open Settlements

Other settlements of the B people are the undefended hamlets and farmsteads in which the occupants lived in stone or timber huts, as for example at Kynance Gate, Lizard. At Bodrifty, the huts of the original settlers were rebuilt in better granite masonry and three acres of surrounding farmland enclosed by a stone wall at this time. In West Penwith other hut groups were started in the middle Iron Age that continued as 'courtyard-house' villages in the Roman period, such as Goldherring or Porthmeor, to be described in the next chapter (p 177).

The famous lake villages of Meare and Glastonbury can be regarded as flourishing outposts of the south-western B culture as well as centres of Iron Age commerce in their own right. They were founded probably in the fourth or third century BC by colonists who arrived by way of

146

the River Brue and the Bristol Channel and who imposed themselves on the local inhabitants of the islands and surrounds of the Somerset fens. The inundations of the first half of the first millennium BC (p 121) were now over and pollen analysis shows that from 450 BC onwards the climate improved and cereal cultivation was resumed.

The results of the prolonged and painstaking—if uninspired—excavations by A. H. Bulleid and H. St George Gray at Glastonbury from 1892 to 1907 have recently been reconsidered by E. K. Tratman. It is now apparent that the original settlement was by people who built small rectangular timber-framed houses, mostly 10ft square, resting on oak piles driven into the peat, three on each side, and secured with mortise and tenon joints. The huts had plank floors, walls of wattlework, probably daubed over, and a thatch roof carried on rafters resting on a ridge pole. Some of them may have been store huts or granaries. Similar houses have been found in the early phase of occupation of hill-forts at Croft Ambrey, Credenhill and Midsummer Hill in the Welsh Marches, and may well be characteristic of an intrusive western group in the early fourth century BC. In central Europe the rectangular house plan is normal in the first part of the Iron Age (Hallstatt D—La Tène I), and the break with the long tradition of round houses in the south-west is significant. The first Glastonbury settlers were good wood-workers, producing lathe-turned bowls and stave-built tubs, and mugs which were probably used instead of pottery. They made vehicles with eight-spoked wheels, and used a horizontal loom for weaving: plough shares, a coulter and querns show that arable cultivation was carried on. Trade with Cornwall is indicated by a sceptre-like tin ingot with gilt-bronze bindings.

There was a complete change in the village during the first century BC when the timber houses were demolished and replaced by round huts. These were built on a foundation of re-used timbers, brushwood and clay, which included much material from the earlier settlement, forming a crannog or artificial island at the edge of open water of the former Meare pool. The two-acre site with its eighty-nine huts was enclosed by a palisade and there was a causeway of clay with a wooden landing stage leading out to a deep-water anchorage. The huts were 18ft to 28ft in diameter, roofed with a centre post and with floors and hearths of clay, which needed frequent renewal due to the compacting and sinking of the underlying strata: as many as ten floor levels were apparent in one hut. The culture and economy were also different: these people were skilled metal-workers, shown by the remains of furnaces, tools and crucibles used for bronze and enamel: they had a flourishing textile industry, using a vertical loom with clay loom weights, spindle whorls and decorated weaving combs made from sheep bones. The emphasis was therefore on pastoral rather than arable farming. They used and probably controlled the manufacture of the decorated pottery in the locality (p 137: Peacock, groups 2–4, Fig 39), which was widely traded in north Somerset. They used Mendip lead for net sinkers and imported Kimmeridge shale from south Dorset to make small objects like bracelets. The village was eventually abandoned due to renewed flooding in the first half of the first century AD.

At the neighbouring Meare village, which consisted of two crannogs each with some sixty round huts, new excavations by M. Avery have revealed a similar sequence, with earlier structures covered by clay deposits. This too was a creative centre with long-distance trading connections. Clear glass beads with attractive inlaid patterns of chrome yellow threads, for example, were made at Meare and reached as far as Pen Dinas hill-fort, near Aberystwyth, and northern Ireland.

THE THIRD PHASE
Iron Age C Intruders

Towards the end of the Iron Age two more small groups of Celtic peoples penetrated separately and to a limited extent into the west and east of the peninsula, one coming from north-west France and the other from Dorset. The former, who will be designated south-western C, were probably refugees from the attacks of Julius Caesar. They used wheel-made and burnished pottery, including large storage jars and wide-mouthed bowls similar to those found in French hill-forts like Le Petit Celland, Manche, and current there in the mid-first century BC.

Such pottery was brought to Britain in the first place by Gallic traders, using southern ports like Hengistbury Head, Mount Batten, or Mounts Bay, whence a little black cordoned pot from Sennen was probably derived. Thereafter it was manufactured in Cornwall by potters using the gabbroitic clays of the Lizard peninsula and distributed to the existing population.

At St Mawgan in Pyder, near the Lanherne tin streams, these new-style wares were found to succeed the decorated B wares and to be associated with a rebuilding of the huts. The settlement was at the end of a low spur, fortified by a single rampart and ditch, and with an in-turned entrance revetted in timber and later rebuilt in stone. The second period huts were 20–30ft in diameter but not truly circular, with an internal post-ring surrounding a central hearth: the floors were levelled into the hillside and at the back there was an earth bank revetted with stone. Hut A, which was attached to another dwelling, Hut W, was a metalworker's workshop; it had two stone-lined hearths in the centre and a long furnace-pit as well as another in a lean-to outside the back of the hut. Tin ore, a bronze ingot and crucibles were found amid much burning on the floor. A fine decorated bronze shield mount (Fig 42) found rolled up as scrap metal, was probably manufactured here at the turn of the first centuries BC–AD. A wide variety of cordoned jars made of gabbroitic clay were in use and were associated with worn decorated B wares in huts and in gullies underlying them, but also with Roman-ised wares in the later levels. About AD 50–70, perhaps at the time of a Roman advance to the west (p 164) the entrance to the fort was re-modelled, some of the huts rebuilt and three new ones constructed: the settlement then continued until the mid-second century AD.

Much cordoned C pottery has been found in recent excavations at the Rumps promontory fort, Polzeath, and sporadically elsewhere in Cornwall and north Devon. At Castle Dore hill-fort it occurred only in the later huts, after the defences and entrance had been remodelled c 50 BC.

The second group who penetrated into south-east Devon were colonists from the Durotriges of Dorset and Somerset. They issued coins (p 151), a large hoard of which was found at Cotley near Axminster

Fig 42 Bronze shield-mount from Carloggas hill-fort, St Mawgan-in-Pyder, Cornwall. Scale 1 :3

and produced wheel-made pottery, of which a bead-rim bowl (Plate 16d) often decorated with three ribs and festoons of dots is characteristic. They also used tall black-burnished cooking pots with upright rims and lattice decoration, jars with counter-sunk lug-handles, mugs and occasionally cordoned and pedestal pottery of Belgic type.

The bulk of the pottery was manufactured in South Dorset where kilns have been found as at Corfe Mullen dating from the first century AD.

At Hembury, the *oppidum* near Honiton (Plate 18b, p 140) these late Iron Age people reduced the size of the fort by building two transverse ramparts and ditches across the centre and living only in the northern half. The west entrance was blocked but there was a gate to the southern tip of the spur through the new defences. Finds show that the occupation continued until about AD 65–70.

TRADE AND CURRENCY IN THE LATE IRON AGE

In the mid first century BC Julius Caesar broke the sea power of the Veneti and Coriosolites, the Armorican tribes who had become the principal carriers of tin from the south-west (p 135). Overseas trade in metals thereafter declined, for the Romans had regained the control of the Spanish mines and the supply to the Mediterranean was assured. Its place was taken in some degree by trade with the neighbouring Celtic confederacies, the Durotriges of Dorset and south Somerset and the Dobunni of Gloucestershire and north Somerset.

The Durotriges had an *entrepôt* within the large promontory fort on Hengistbury Head, which controlled the Stour and Salisbury Avon waterways. Excavations in 1912 by J. P. Bushe-Fox showed that silver and copper coins were minted here, metals were smelted, shale worked, and several varieties of continental pottery imported in the first centuries BC and AD. The coins were debased copies of the gold stater of Philip of Macedon, which had reached southern Britain from Belgic Gaul early in the first century BC; the Durotrigian model was the Gaulish Atrebatic stater (Allen's Gallo-Belgic C.), from which the head and horse designs on obverse and reverse were reduced to a series of dots and squiggles by the native moneyers. Twelve newly minted Durotrigian silver coins were found in the large hoard of Armorican coins at Le Câtillon in Jersey, deposited *c* 56–51 BC showing that the Durotriges were striking in the first half of the first century BC. Whilst the design of the coins came from the south-east, the metal was derived from the south-west. Analysis of a 19lb block of silver alloy from one of the furnaces at Hengistbury by Professor Gowland proved it to be derived from an argentiferous copper ore obtainable in the Callington district. Further proof of a Durotrigian trading connection with the Dumnonii comes from Mount Batten, Plymouth, where silver coins occur in the settlement and in hoards with others of the Coriosolites.

The Dobunni also traded with the Dumnonii. Their uninscribed gold and silver staters, with the characteristic triple tailed horse on the reverse and fernlike symbol on the obverse occur at Mount Batten, and single examples of their inscribed issues of the first century AD have been recorded from Plymouth, Bellever Tor on Dartmoor and Camborne, Cornwall. The trade route was down the Stour to Hengistbury and by the south coast. Its earlier use is shown by finds of iron currency bars, which were extensively used by the western B peoples of the Severn–Cotswold area, and reached both Hengistbury and south Devon; a hoard of twelve bars was found at a small hill-fort in Holne Chase, in the same metalliferous district on the Dart as the two Greek silver coins were found (p 135).

A trading connection with the Belgic settlement in Kent is indicated by the surviving uninscribed coins from two hoards found in 1749 in Carn Brea hill-fort, Camborne, which was well situated to control the tin of Penwith; a single coin of Cunobelin (AD 5–40), the Belgic ruler of the south-east, was also found here.

The Dumnonii themselves never achieved a coinage: it is possible that they, like the Masai in East Africa, counted their wealth in cattle and used the beasts to fix a bride-price and as a medium of exchange amongst themselves.

CELTIC ART AND RELIGION

The excellence of decorative metalwork produced by the Celtic peoples in Britain before the Roman conquest is well known, and it remains to assess the south-western achievements in this respect. There is nothing in the region that can be assigned to the first flowering of insular La Tène art in the third century BC, which developed from continental models in the Waldalgesheim style and was strongly influenced by the classical palmette, seen on the Thames and Witham shields. The nearest examples are two minor pieces, the bronze spoons or scoops from Weston near Bath, and the bit-rings from West Coker, Yeovil, which both have derivative spidery designs in low relief. In the peninsula at this time the population was

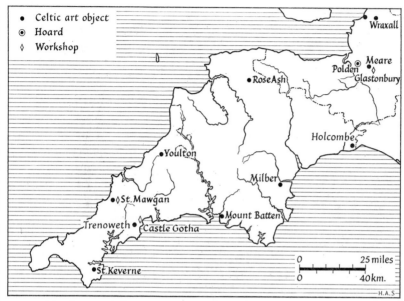

Fig 43 Distribution of Celtic art objects and workshops

unsettled, and neither the craftsmen nor the market for finery stabilised.

The first century BC saw the establishment of schools of metal-workers in southern Britain, producing articles for chieftains and their women decorated in accordance with local tastes and changing fashions. Bronze working in huts at Glastonbury and Meare, at Castle Gotha and at St Mawgan-in-Pyder have already been mentioned, which together with recent finds of metal-workers' hearths and tools at South Cadbury hill-fort, Somerset, indicate that the craft was widespread. It must not be assumed, however, that all metalwork found in the south-west was made locally; some may have been produced by itinerant smiths; others may be trade goods or gifts which have travelled far from their place of origin. The distribution of fine pieces is scattered with a concentration in north Somerset, an area with a long tradition of bronze working.

153

The Western 'Mirror School'

The south-western region can claim to be the origin of the British 'mirror style', so called from the engraved decoration on the backs of mirrors found in women's graves both in the west and the Belgic south-east, *c* AD 0–50. The patterns are linear, incised in outline on the bronze with the aid of a compass and then worked over with a tracer; parts were infilled by chased vertical and horizontal lines arranged in panels, making a basketry pattern. Favourite motifs were the pelta, a triangle with two concave and one convex curved sides, and a crescent or crescent-ring filled with radial hatching as on the Holcombe mirror (Plate 20a). The earliest example is on a sword scabbard found in peat cutting on Meare Heath in 1928 (Fig 44) and which is dated by its heart-shaped chape to the early first century BC. The design on the locket is balanced but asymmetrical; the ambiguity between the background and pattern is characteristic. The St Keverne mirror (Plate 20b), from a woman's grave in an inhumation cemetery at Trelan Bahow in the Lizard, is recognisably in the same style; its two engraved roundels contain different asymmetrical designs, but composed of the same elements: it probably dates from the late first century BC. The unprovenanced 'Mayer' mirror in the Liverpool Museum with three linked roundels is of the same queer type and another early example of this western school; Sir Cyril Fox has shown that its design is ancestral to the whole of the British mirror series.

o ___ *1 in.*

Fig 44 Bronze scabbard mount ornament from Meare, Somerset

The finest of the western mirrors were made just before the Roman conquest: at Holcombe, Uplyme, a superb example (Plate 20a) was found buried in a pit in a small enclosed settlement, dated by Durotrigian pottery (p 150) to the first half of the first century AD. The engraved design is symmetrical, reflecting the influence of classical silver of the Augustan era (23 BC–AD 14). The mirror was probably designed to be suspended from the loop at the end of the handle, because when inverted, the red-studded mount can be seen to be a stylised feline face: such hidden images are a well-known feature of Celtic art. The engraved design and the basketry technique closely resemble those of the famous Birdlip mirror from a woman's grave on the edge of the Cotswolds, near Gloucester, which was dated by associated finds to the first century AD. Other mirrors from burials at Mount Batten (Stamford Hill), Plymouth, the Verne, Portland, and from Nijmegen, Holland, are products of the same western school of engraving judging by their limited range of identical motifs.

Pieces by the same metal-smiths can also be identified in the hoard of harness trappings and armour found in 1803 at Knowle Bawdrip on the Polden ridge in north Somerset. They include two heavy brooches, one engraved and one enamelled, that were probably used to fasten a horse's caparison, as well as a set of bits and rein-rings (terrets) with pelta designs with a stippled in-filling.

The handsome bronze collar from Wraxall, Somerset, and the shield-mount from St Mawgan-in-Pyder (Fig 42) show the more florid relief decoration, which was practised by another western school in the early first century AD. Running scrolls and peltae high-lighted with spots of glass or enamel are characteristic motifs, stippling replaces basketry as infilling, and a wavy line produced by alternating fine punch marks was often employed. The bronze collar found in a tin stream at Trenoweth, St Stephen-in-Brannell, is a product of a less competent craftsman of this school; the decoration consists of stippled peltas flanked by squat trumpet scrolls, which retain their insets of clear and amber glass; the design is a simplification of that on the Wraxall collar from north Somerset. It is made in two parts of thin sheet bronze beaten over and riveted at either end to a lead core. The fastening is uncertain; the analogous Wraxall collar swivels on and fastens by ingenious mortise and tenon joints. Two others very similar have been found in south Dorset, so the Cornish collar may have reached the tin area in the course of trade along the south coast. Such collars are too heavy for regular wear and probably were for ceremonial use: they may have adorned an image like the torc shown on the bronze statue of the Gallic god from Bouray, Seine et Oise, and on many others. The small wooden idol found in the clay works at Hennock in the lower Teign valley, though not closely dateable, shows that human cult figures were known in the south-west (Plate 21b).

Two bronze bowls from Rose Ash, north Devon and from Youlton, north Cornwall may also be associated with religious observances; both were found in bogs and like the famous silver cauldron from Gundestrup, Denmark, or the Llyn Cerrig hoard in Anglesey, were probably votive offerings. The bowls are made of thin beaten bronze with the rims finished by turning on a lathe and decorated by characteristic south-western wavy lines. The Rose Ash bowl has an animal-head escutcheon (Plate 17a), probably an ox, Youlton has an inverted human or daemonic head, probably wearing a plumed helmet: like the Holcombe mirror handle they illustrate the Celtic capacity for formalising imagery. The bowls date from the end of the first century BC and the beginning of the first century AD: two others were found in the rich woman's grave at Birdlip, Glos, with the fine mirror and grave-goods of 1–15 AD whilst others travelled far afield to Keshcarrigan on the Shannon and to Leg Piekarski in central Poland, where one was placed in a chieftain's grave in the late first century AD. Such exports are a tribute to the excellence of the western metal smiths.

CHAPTER VIII

The Roman Canton
of the Dumnonii

THE MILITARY OCCUPATION AD 45–80
The Roman armies of the Emperor Claudius reached the south-west
at the conclusion of their victorious campaign against the Durotriges
and the western Belgic tribes. A task force comprising the Second
Augustan Legion and auxiliaries under the command of the *legatus
legionis*, the future emperor Vespasian, had stormed some twenty hill-
forts, Maiden Castle amongst them, and conquered the Isle of Wight.
The Dumnonii probably soon submitted, thus freeing the military command to move north-east against the Dobunni in north Somerset and
Gloucester with their rear secure. By AD 47–48 the initial conquest of
the West Country was practically complete, a fort had been founded at
Exeter, the important silver and lead mining district on the Mendips
was occupied and a military road, the Fossway, had been engineered to
link up with other army groups away to the north-east. A wide zone
of military occupation formed the frontier at this time, extending westwards from the forts at Hod and Wadden Hill in south Dorset to the
Exe and north-eastwards through Cirencester, Leicester and Lincoln
to the Humber.

The Fossway (Fig 45) itself is a striking example of a Roman road
and much of the south-western sector survives and is used by traffic
today. Starting from Exeter the road was aligned north-east so as to
avoid the Somerset marshes, the fringes of which were crossed on a high

agger (embankment) at Ilchester. Thereafter it followed a direct course across undulating country to the Avon at Bath, aligned in characteristic long straight stretches from sighting points on hill-tops. A section uncovered at Ilchester showed that it was constructed on a foundation of the local lias rock which had been packed with flinty gravel and lime mortar and surfaced with fine gravel to a width of over 14ft.

At Exeter a short length of the defences of a fort was found in South Street in 1964, occupying some six acres of level ground south of the later Roman city (Fig 48). These consisted of a characteristic V-shaped ditch, 8ft wide, and the base of a timber-faced rampart. Wedged in the ditch bottom there was the neck of a 'Rhodian' type amphora, an imported wine jar of the mid-first century AD. The fort was tactically well placed to command a crossing of the nearby river at the head of tidal

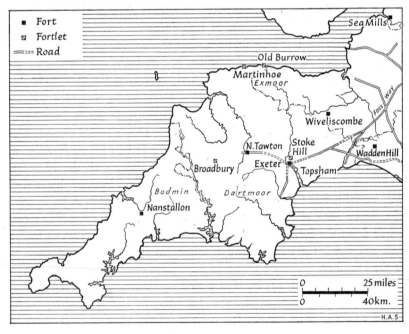

Fig 45 Map of Roman military sites

water and to control traffic to and from the east by the Fossway. It was supplemented by a fortlet as a look-out post and signal station on the 500ft crest of Stoke Hill, with extensive views north and west over the Creedy and Exe valleys. Other garrison forts in this sector of the frontier have yet to be discovered (Fig 45): Ilchester, where the Fossway was joined by a road from mid Dorset, is a probable site, although the mid-first-century settlement within the later Roman town walls appears to be native in character.

After AD 47, when Ostorius Scapula succeeded Aulus Plautius, Claudius' first governor and commander-in-chief, the frontier was menaced by the Silures, the Celtic tribes in South Wales, who were skilfully led by Caractacus, the refugee Belgic ruler. An advanced legionary base therefore was established to control the Severn crossing at Gloucester for the Twentieth brought up from Colchester.

It is probable that about this time a detachment of the Second Augustan legion was moved forward from Dorset to Exeter and occupied the centre of the later city (Fig 48). Recent excavations have found remains of long timber buildings behind the Guildhall which may be barracks, and opposite the cathedral, part of a magnificent stone bath building which, if the early date can be substantiated, can only be legionary work. The discovery of the defences of a fortress on the central plateau site are needed to prove this hypothesis; elaborate bath buildings are known to have been erected inside the first-century legionary fortresses at Caerleon and Chester. The interior finish of the military baths at Exeter was of a high order: in the *caldarium* which measured 40ft across, there were moulded panels of Purbeck marble veneered on the walls, a stone imported from south Dorset and large hot water basins of the same stone in the twin apses resting on a tiled base. The floors were either mosaic or of *opus signinum*, a composition of pounded tile and cement, resting on a thick concrete bedding which retained the heat from the underfloor hypocaust, in which hot air from the furnace circulated round the supporting pillars *(pilæ)* of red tiles. The roof had decorative tile antefixes with grotesque faces of the winds in relief.

Remains of timber houses found in South Street in 1945–6 can now be re-interpreted in the light of the new discoveries as houses for the officers of the legion, the tribunes, the camp-prefect or even the commander *(legatus legionis)*. The houses were aligned on either side of a metalled road with a central drain, probably the *via principalis*, leading down-hill to the river crossing. They were constructed with a framework of stout posts 2–3ft apart with walls of interwoven wattle and daub and with tile roofs. One had a veranda facing on to an internal courtyard, and included a kitchen with much domestic refuse, later used as a workshop. Some furnaces found in Bartholomew Street in 1959 may indicate the site of the *fabrica* or legionary workshops.

With the legionary headquarters established at Exeter, it is likely that the military occupied zone was extended farther westwards to the Bristol Channel to forestall a Silurian landing on the flank (Fig 45). Sea Mills *(Abonæ)* near Avonmouth at which many Claudian coins and some early Samian pottery have been found, was occupied at this time, making a harbour in the Avon available to the fleet. An undated 3½-acre fort at Wiveliscombe, north-west of Taunton, has been tentatively assigned to this period. At Topsham there are finds indicative of a port on the Exe estuary in pre-Flavian times, which was perhaps a naval supply base working in conjunction with the Exeter legionary fortress.

A watch on the Silures proved to be necessary for the next twenty years until they were finally subdued by Julius Frontinus, the governor, in AD 74–75. For this purpose two fortlets were built successively on high points on the Exmoor coast at Old Burrow and Martinhoe (Fig 46) on either side of Lynmouth, which command extensive views across the channel to South Wales. Both were strongly defended by double ramparts and ditches with a third line about 70ft away forming an outer enclosure. The single entrances were on opposite sides so that if attackers forced the outer gate, they would have to make a half circuit under fire between the defences before reaching the gate of the inner enclosure. The fortlets were built and maintained by troops who probably were landed in the nearby coves on the rocky coast: the isolated garrisons would need to establish friendly relations with the native peoples in the many small hill-forts in the neighbourhood.

17a *(above)* Bronze bowl, Rose Ash, North Devon. Diameter 7·5in. British Museum 17b *(below)* Tin ingot, Fal estuary, St Mawes, Cornwall. Length 2ft 10in, weight 158lb. Truro Museum

18a *(above)* Trevelgue
promontory fort, Newquay,
Cornwall
18b *(left)* Hembury
hill-fort, Payhembury,
East Devon

Excavations at Old Burrow have shown that it was a Claudian construction and that Martinhoe was occupied in the reign of Nero (AD 54–68); it seems unlikely that the fortlet was evacuated before Frontinus' successful Welsh campaigns of AD 74–75. The garrison was a detachment of eighty men (a century), who were housed in two wooden barracks (Fig 46), divided into cubicles with extra rooms in one of them for the officer-in-charge. Their cooking was done in a row of field ovens at the back of the turf rampart; a third building, which had a small domed furnace outside it, was probably for the armourers. Signal fires on the cliff edge in the outer enclosure show how these outposts gave

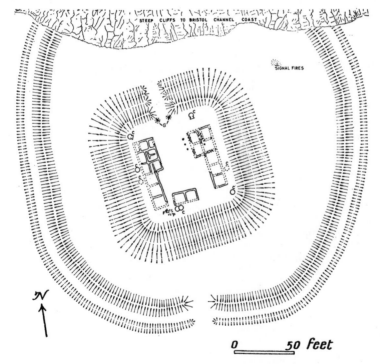

Fig 46 Reconstructed plan of the Roman fortlet of Martinhoe, north Devon. C, ovens; F, furnace; G, post-holes for gate posts; P, pit

warning of enemy movement across the Bristol Channel, visible from their high vantage points. The signals would be directed to ships of the Roman fleet ready to intercept.

During the reign of Nero the Roman army once again took the offensive against the Dumnonii and advanced into mid-Cornwall, where they established a fort at Nanstallon on the River Camel, west of Bodmin. The occasion for this is not known; it could be that the Dumnonii had given trouble in AD 60–61 during the rebellion of Boudicca and the Iceni, it could be that a decision was taken earlier by the governor to gain control of the peninsula and its mineral resources for the emperor.

The two-acre fort at Nanstallon (Fig 47) has been well excavated and provides a picture of the Roman army on garrison work. The unit was probably not legionary, but an auxiliary unit, a *cohors equitata quingenaria*, comprising 380 infantry and 120 cavalry troops, The soldiers were housed in wooden barracks, six to eight men sharing a double cubicle with more spacious quarters for the centurions or decurions at one end. The commander had a spacious house (the *praetorium*) near the east gate of the fort with a large dining room *(triclinium)* at the rear suitable for entertaining the local chiefs. Adjoining it in the centre of the fort there was the headquarters building *(principia)* which had a colonnaded front and internal courtyard. The granaries and stores must be situated in the western half of the fort, which was not excavated. The fort itself was defended by a turf rampart and ditch and by four timber angle towers and double gates, and was occupied until AD 75–80.

Other forts in Cornwall are yet to be found: in west Devon (Fig 45) there is a possible half-acre fortlet on the crest of Broadbury, 800ft on a ridge road aiming to cross the Tamar above Launceston, and at North Tawton there is a rectangular earthwork with an annexe which is of the right proportions for a $6\frac{1}{2}$ acre auxiliary fort; some first-century Roman pottery has been found here. The fort is sited to control a crossing of the Taw and has a four-mile straight stretch of road on its east side across the claylands followed by parish boundaries. These sites indicate that the Roman route to the west from the Exeter headquarters lay to the north of Dartmoor and Bodmin Moor. Native opposition to

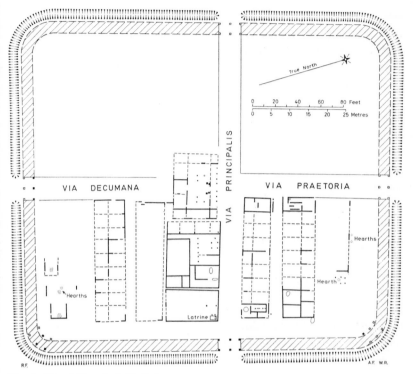

Fig 47 Nanstallon fort, Bodmin

the Roman advance is evident at St Mawgan-in-Pyder (p 149) where the
gate to the hill-fort was refortified at this time.

Although the military occupation of the peninsula lasted until the
end of the reign of Vespasian (AD 69–79), there must have been a change
of garrison at Exeter when the Second Augustan legion moved to
Gloucester to replace the Twentieth legion, which was transferred to
Wroxeter in AD 67. Some of the barracks in the Guildhall site were
altered at this time and new timber buildings were put up along a road
on the Batholomew Street site in place of the military workshops. The
caldarium of the great baths was reduced in size, indicative of a smaller
garrison. Some buildings may even have been converted for civilian

use. By AD 80 the military situation had changed fundamentally: the need was now for troops to garrison Wales and for campaigns in the north. Consequently the territory of the Dumnonii was evacuated.

THE FOUNDATION AND DEVELOPMENT OF ISCA DUMNONIORUM, c AD 80–85

Exeter now developed as a self-governing Roman town in accordance with the governor Agricola's (AD 78–89) declared policy of encouraging native urban development and the romanisation of the inhabitants. The officers' houses and the road in South Street were demolished and the site levelled for a large gravelled *piazza* with surrounding ambulatory which was probably part of the forum (Fig 48). The great bath building, which was still standing, was converted probably into municipal offices; it was given a new monumental entrance, a doorway flanked by columns at the top of a flight of steps. New walls were inserted into the *caldarium*, making it into a set of three rooms, the underfloor heating having been demolished and packed solid with rubble and clay. A row of small shops was built alongside it, fronting on to an east to west road, which was beneath the later St Mary Major church. A new set of Public Baths was built on the opposite side of this road where the Deanery now stands: a portico and a plunge bath of which a paved surround in the *frigidarium* were located in 1932, and a stone-lined conduit for waste water in Bear Street in 1954. From the second century onwards, houses in the city were built in stone, with cement or tessellated floors, some with simple geometric designs, but which were only rarely heated by hypocausts. Trade flourished, as shown by the imports of second-century Samian pottery from Lezoux, and by a number of Roman coins with Greek legends from eastern Mediterranean mints, mostly Alexandrian tetradrachms of the third century AD when this mint was prolific in its issues.

Up till the middle of the second century AD the city, like most others in Britain, was unenclosed and undefended: a rampart and ditch was constructed about AD 160 enclosing ninety-two acres (Fig 48), to which an impressive stone wall (Plate 22) was added some time after AD 200.

166

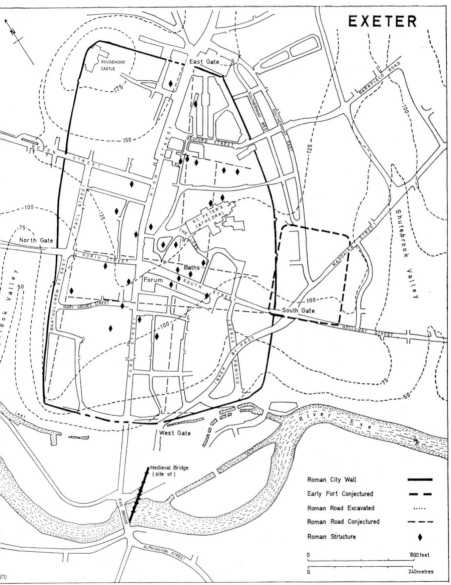

Fig 48 *Roman sites in Exeter*

167

It was built of the local dark volcanic stone, with a core of grouted rubble 10ft thick and a facing of ashlar above a chamfered plinth. There were four gates, all rebuilt in medieval times and finally removed in the early nineteenth century. Excavations in 1964 at the South Gate uncovered a 16ft square tower of Roman masonry on the west side of the entrance, which was probably through a central archway flanked by separate footways. The defences, like those of the majority of British town walls, were undertaken probably in accordance with an edict of the Emperor Septimius Severus (AD 199–211) in consequence of the serious disturbances in the province at the end of the second century, or of his successors in the first half of the third century AD. In its heyday, *Isca* must have been an attractive city, unusual in that so much of its interior was on steeply sloping ground with views to the neighbouring hills.

The importance of *Isca* was not only that of a self-contained town in which the pleasures of a civilised life were available to its inhabitants in an attractive and secure urban setting, but, as its name with the tribal suffix implies, it was the administrative centre for the whole of the Dumnonian people, the *Civitas Dumnoniorum*. Under the Roman scheme for the Celtic peoples who had strong tribal loyalties, the Iron Age confederacies were constituted self-governing units, run on the new democratic pattern, each with a principal city. At *Isca Dumnoniorum*, the *ordo* or Council composed of the decurions and their elected magistrates, drawn in the first instance from the tribal chieftains, would discuss matters that concerned not only the town but the whole of the penin-

Fig 49 Inscriptions of the Dumnonii from Carvoran and Thirwall on Hadrian's Wall

sula. The Council were responsible for the assessment and collection of taxes throughout the canton, both those levied on the *civitas* by the Imperial procurator on behalf of the central government and those required locally. Two inscriptions on Hadrian's Wall (Fig 49) attest a corporate act of the *Civitas Dumnoniorum*, in company of other *civitates*, a contribution in men or money, towards the rebuilding of the northern frontier in Severan times or in the fourth century.

THE CANTON

The territory governed from *Isca* extended westward for the length of the Cornish peninsula as is evident from Ptolemy's naming of the Lizard as the Dumnonian promontory. On the east, the boundary with the Durotriges lay in the tumbled-wooded country at the end of the Blackdowns traversed by the Fossway. It then extended north-east from the Parrett, for the Somerset River Axe apparently was included in Dumnonian territory by Ptolemy writing in the second century AD, and as we have seen (p 137) this district had strong cultural links with the peninsula in the Iron Age. Some adjustment was probably effected in the third century when Ilchester *(Lindinis)* was recognised as a cantonal town of the *Civitas Durotrigensis*, in addition to Dorchester *(Durnovaria)*. The flourishing population in the villas on the land fringing the Somerset marsh in late Roman times must relate to this township, not to *Isca* (Fig 50).

Roads

The canton was served by a road system initiated and maintained by the central government, which linked it with the rest of the province. *Isca* was reached by the Fossway (Fig 50) and by a new branch road from Dorchester *(Durnovaria)* of which good stretches are preserved between Axminster and Honiton and at Rockbeare. West of the Exe, a road with *agger* and side ditches has recently been traced over Haldon, which crossed the Teign by a bridge above Newton Abbot to serve south Devon, whilst north of Dartmoor, the length of road at North Tawton already mentioned (p 164) aimed for the Tamar on its way to

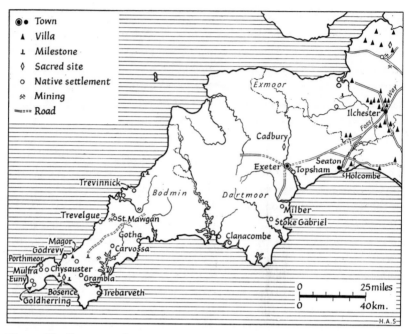

Fig 50 The Roman south-west

the west: as today, Dartmoor compelled a divide in the main roads at
Exeter. In Cornwall no constructed roads have been identified with
certainty but five milestones of the mid-third and early fourth centuries
show that it was included in the system, probably when tin mining was
resumed in late imperial times (p 183). Those at Tintagel and Boscastle
and at St Hilary and Breage are evidence for short lengths on the north
and south coast respectively, whilst the Gwennap Pit milestone of
Gordian III, found upright and probably *in situ* near Redruth, could
relate to a road down the spine of the narrowing peninsula. Traffic must
also have been by sea, principally along the south coast as in prehistoric
times.

The limited knowledge of the road system prevents us from making
use of the road-books to identify the principal places in the canton.

The second century Antonine Itinerary mentions *Moridunum*, a town 15 miles from Exeter and 36 from Dorchester, which should be in the Otter valley, whilst the Ravenna Cosmography, a compilation of early road-books in the seventh century, mentions it on a route east from Exeter *(Scadummorum)* to Ilchester *(Lindinis)*. The Cosmography also contains a string of 14 place-names, mostly unidentifiable, but situated to the west of Exeter; they include *Tamaris,* which must be at a crossing of the Tamar, preceded by *Nemetostatio,* which on the evidence of the present-day *Nymet* names around Bow and North Tawton is probably the North Tawton fort (p 164): the suffix *statio* implies that it became a tax-collecting centre. A second *statio, Deventiasteno* was probably in south Devon, perhaps at Mount Batten or Plymouth.

Roman-style Buildings

A new centre for administration, new building techniques, and a new relationship to a power outside the area fostered by new lines of communication were, then, the principal introductions of Roman rule. To what extent did they affect the life of the Dumnonii and how far did their territory become romanised? There can be no simple answer to these questions. The transition from the Celtic to the Romano-British way of life can sometimes be traced archaeologically when a round hut was replaced by a mortared stone house as at Catsgore in Somerset. Among the Dumnonii the first steps can be seen at Milber, Newton Abbot, where a rectangular enclosure for the wooden buildings of a native farm was erected *c* AD 50 beside an abandoned concentric hill-fort. Similarly the peoples living in Hembury hill-fort (p 150) moved away about AD 70 after having acquired some Romano-British goods, but their new settlement is undiscovered.

Roman-style buildings in the canton are few and with one exception are limited to east Devon (Fig 50); even in the pleasant Exe valley, within easy reach of *Isca* and the new roads, or in hinterland of Torbay, no villas are recorded, which is puzzling. On Seaton Down, overlooking the Axe estuary, extensive remains of stone buildings with tessellated floors and hypocausts were uncovered in the nineteenth century. Recent excavations have revealed a complex of early timber buildings, a small detached bath house, an aisled building and a road of two periods. Their character is consistent with either a large country-house with outbuildings or more likely with a small township. This may be *Moridunum*, for the Latin place-name given in the *Itinerary*, a second-century road book appropriately means 'the fort by the sea', which in Saxon speech could have become Seaton. But if the distances in the *Itinerary* are correct *Moridunum* should be a settlement ten miles nearer to Exeter.

At Holcombe, Uplyme, it appears that there was continuity of land-holding from late Iron Age times right through the Roman period, apart from a short interval at the time of the Conquest when the decorated bronze mirror was hidden (Plate 20). About AD 80 a timber-framed aisled house was built inside the ditched enclosure, replacing the late Iron Age round huts. The owner used Samian and new-style Roman wares as well as the Durotrigian black-burnished pottery. More rooms and a veranda were added built in stone during the second and third centuries as well as a timber barn over the filled-in ditch. In the early fourth century the villa was again extended to include an octagonal bath house of unusual design: it had a central stepped plunge bath, 3ft deep, with a blue and white key-patterned tessellated surround, stone columns, corbels and a pendentive decorated with patterns of carved scallop shells, all indicative of a building of some architectural distinction. Another room had a mosaic floor 18ft square with an unusual geometric design in three colours, which was carefully recorded in the early nineteenth century. The bath suite at Lufton, near Yeovil, which has an attractive mosaic of fishes surrounding the octagonal plunge, is probably a work of the same West Country architect among the Durotriges. The only other recorded remains of well-built country houses are from Combe St Nicholas and Whitestaunton on the Devon-Somerset border.

That there was luxurious living in the Roman style in east Devon is shown by the fine bronze mount from a tripod found in 1840 on the beach at Sidmouth (Plate 21a): it figures the boy Achilles riding

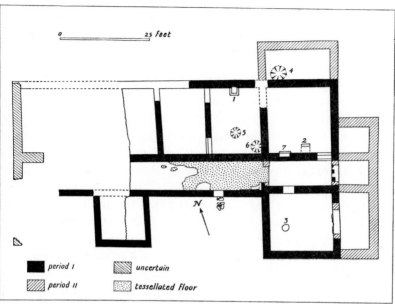

Fig 51 Plan of the Roman villa at Magor, Camborne, Cornwall. 1–3, hearths; 4–6, pits; 7, wall recess

Cheiron the centaur and hunting a wild beast and is a Mediterranean import of the second century AD. Such tripods supported either bronze bowls or small table tops when the evening meal was served in a well-to-do household.

The one Roman style building remote from *Isca* is the small country house at Magor, near Camborne in west Cornwall, which was erected in the mid-second century, extended and abandoned in the third century (Fig 51). The house possesses in a crude form most of the novelties in building technique: a slate roof, mortared walls lined with painted plaster, a tessellated floor in the corridor and others of cement or *opus signinum*. Its rusticity is betrayed by its lack of symmetry and by the fact that none of its angles is true: the mason was obviously not acquainted with the rule of Pythagoras. It has been suggested that it was the dwelling of a native of the district who had lived further east, perhaps serving

173

as a decurion in *Isca* or with the army, and who on his return built a house on his estate with local labour in the style which he had become accustomed to see in the town.

Native-Style Buildings

For the majority of the Dumnonii there was little change in their mode of life; they continued to live in small groups in round stone huts and the only signs of contact with a new order were their acquisition of some better-made black cooking pots and dishes, and the occasional coin or trinket. A homestead at Stoke Gabriel, near Totnes, may be taken as typical; here a small community built a rectangular stone-walled cattle pound on a limestone hill-top in the first century AD and continued to live in round huts and to till their small lynchetted fields until the middle of the fourth century. They acquired some Samian and colour-coated wares from a distant market but used mainly rough cook-ing-pots and storage-jars of local manufacture. In west Cornwall the two small enclosed homesteads of Porth and Crane Godrevy, Gwithian, tell the same story. The pottery and a few late third-century coins from the single hut at Porth Godrevy show that it was occupied from the second until the fourth century AD, but the inhabitants had little metal apart from one fine brooch, and were using beach pebbles and stone tools.

The Dumnonii, however, had seen the Roman army construct their rectangular forts as at Nanstallon (Fig 47) with straight metalled roads and timber buildings aligned along them. To a limited extent they imitated them by digging straight lengths of ramparts and ditches in their settlements as at Carvossa, Probus or Trevinnick, St Kew, though they did not succeed in making all the angles true. Carvossa was ob-viously an important place, five acres in extent, strongly fortified and with metalled roads. It was occupied from about AD 60–150: the in-habitants used much native pottery from the Lizard and obtained some imported Samian ware, jugs and *mortaria*. It may be the settlement known to Ptolemy as *Voliba*. Trevinnick, St Kew and Grambla, Wen-dron, are typical of the smaller rectilinear settlements, each about an acre in extent and occupied in the first and second centuries. Clana-combe, near Thurlestone, is a similar rectangular enclosure in south Devon with pottery of c AD 200 in the ditch. These homesteads may be regarded as the Roman period development of the Round (p 145), though many of those of Iron Age origin continued unaltered in outline to a late date, for example St Mawgan-in-Pyder (p 149) and the Round at Castle Gotha (p 146) which were occupied throughout the first and second centuries, without any apparent change in the mode of life. Some of the western hill-forts continued to be inhabited; Carn Brea and Trevelgue have both produced late imperial issues as well as first-century coins, whilst at Norton Fitzwarren (p 112) a quantity of Romano-British pottery shows that occupation continued into the second century.

Courtyard Houses

There is one new development in native architecture in Roman times which is limited to the granitic uplands of Land's End, known to the ancient writers as Belerion: here a house and its outbuildings were built as a single incorporated unit around an open courtyard from which the type is named. It is best seen at Chysauster, Gulval (Fig 52), a village of eight such houses, arranged in pairs on opposite sides of a street, with two or three more together with an underground store (fogou) a short distance away. The houses are irregular ovals, up to 90ft long, terraced into the hillside, with the entrances turned away from the prevailing south-west winds. Across the courtyard was the principal dwelling (3) a round or oval hut with the roof supported on posts set in stone sockets. On one side of the courtyard was a long narrow room (2) which was a work-room, sometimes for industrial purposes, and on the other there was a recess with a lean-to roof (4), probably a stable for ponies. There may also be other small round rooms opening into the courtyard but the round room, long room and courtyard are the constant features of the type. To a certain extent, it reflects the provincial Roman house with its range of separate rooms for different use but the absence of rectangularity shows that it was not a direct copy. Its affinities are more with the round huts at Bodrifty or on Dean Moor (Fig 28) which have internal divisions or with the metal-worker's hut at Kestor (Fig 30) with its central opening dividing the living-room from the smithy.

The inhabitants of Chysauster were primarily farmers; there are lynchetted and terraced fields around the settlement. Each house had a small paddock or garden, whilst a sunk road leads down to the stream for watering stock (Plate 23a). Some water, however, was brought to the village in slab-covered channels, which also act as drains for surface water in the courtyards. The pottery, mostly native copies of Romano-British types but also a few cordoned sherds (p 149) indicates an occupation in the first and second centuries AD and in some houses until the third, when the village was peacefully abandoned.

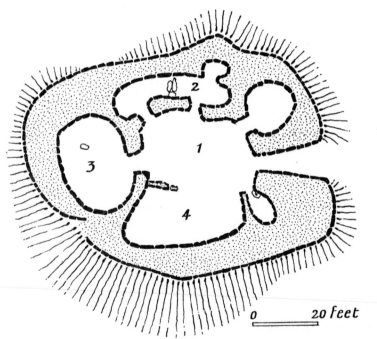

Fig 52 Plan of a courtyard house in the Chysauster settlement, Cornwall. 1, courtyard; 2, long room; 3, round room; 4, stable

There are between thirty and forty examples of these compounds in the Land's End peninsula but they are part of complex village settlements which originated in the late Iron Age. Mulfra Vean, Madron (Fig. 50), has produced cordoned (C) pottery of pre-Roman origin from a courtyard house, which continued to be occupied until the late second or third century AD. At Goldherring, Sancreed, the primary settlement was in round huts enclosed by a stone-faced rampart and ditch: the inhabitants also used late Iron Age cordoned (C) pottery. The courtyard house and associated fields were later, being built in the third century after the site had been abandoned for a while. Occupation then continued into the fifth century, using only native wares including some shallow platters of post-Roman date. At Porthmeor, Zennor, the settlement consisted of seven round huts and two courtyard houses within a walled enclosure of an acre and a second complex, more ruined, with a fogou and another courtyard house lower down the hillside. Here, too, a courtyard house and its associated cultivation terrace were stratigraphically later than the enclosure wall, and were dated by two second-century Roman coins, one of Marcus Aurelius (AD 160–180) sealed in the lower floor of the Round room. The finds from Porthmeor which include some imported red ware (p 191) indicate an occupation of over 400 years, continuing into the fifth century.

Iron or tin smelting was in evidence at Porthmeor: in the Long Room of one courtyard house there was a stone-edged hearth three feet in diameter, the centre lined with sherds to absorb and retain the heat, which rested on a cone of burnt clay probably from a previous smelt, whilst in the Round room of the second house, there was another pottery-lined hearth with a forging pit beside it, two feet deep and full of fire rakings.

Fogous

Another feature peculiar to the Land's End settlements is the provision of a *souterrain* or underground chamber, known locally as a *fogou*. These may be entered from one of the courtyard houses as at Carn Euny, Sancreed (Plate 23b), or be situated a little distance away as at

Chysauster. There are a few fogous built inside small defensible earthworks as at Treveneague, St Hilary, but they never occur at the large contour or promontory forts. They were constructed by excavating a sloping trench about 5ft wide and 6ft deep, lining it with drystone walling which was battered inwards and roofed with flat slabs: the soil from the excavation was heaped on top as at Pendeen Vau or incorporated in the rampart of the enclosure as at Halligey, Trelowarren. The usual plan (Fig 53) is a curving gallery with entrances at either end and orientated south-west–north-east, facing the prevailing wind; there may also be shafts and side-chambers as at Boleigh or Carn Euny. At Porthmeor (p 177) a similar structure was built above ground, curving round the Round room of a courtyard house, and contemporary with it.

Analogous constructions are found in eastern Scotland where they are also associated with hut groups as at Ardestie, Angus, in Ireland and in Brittany. The functions of these structures have been much debated: when Hencken wrote in 1932, it was assumed that they were hiding-places, with an emergency exit through the end or side passages in case of trouble, despite the fact that the main entrance is obvious and that the majority would be death-traps in an attack. It now seems likely they were for domestic use, and were built as communal cellars or cold stores. Food stored in them would be kept at an even temperature, being below ground, in a through draught and free from contamination by flies: meat could be dried in them as was done until very recently in passage-like drystone buildings in Shetland, where after the autumn killing, skinned and gutted carcases were hung on stretchers in the drying-house for several months. The ashpits found at Trewardreva fogou and in the circular side-chamber at Carn Euny probably were for preserving gulls' eggs, as was done on St Kilda until recently. The deep layer of black greasy mould with charcoal, animal and bird bones which covered the floor at Treveneague is also suggestive of a food store. Finally there is the statement of Diodorus Siculus that Iron Age people in Britain stored their grain in 'underground repositories', bringing out a little for grinding each day; since this information was derived

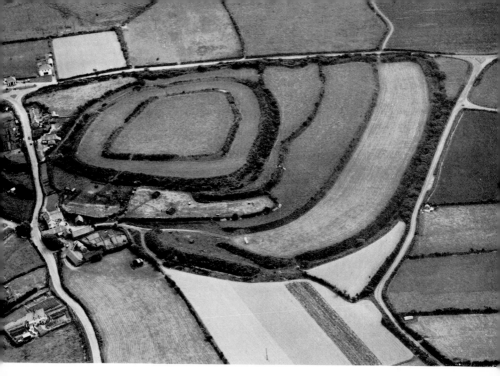

Hill-forts of south-western type. 19a *(above)* Clovelly Dykes hill-fort, Clovelly, North Devon 19b *(below)* Prestonbury hill-fort, Drewsteignton, Devon

Decorated bronze mirrors of the late Iron Age.
20a *(left)* Holcombe, Uplyme, East Devon. British Museum
20b *(below)* Trelan Bahow, St Keverne, Cornwall. British Museum

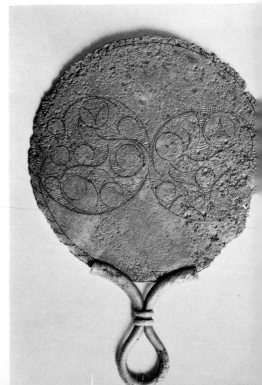

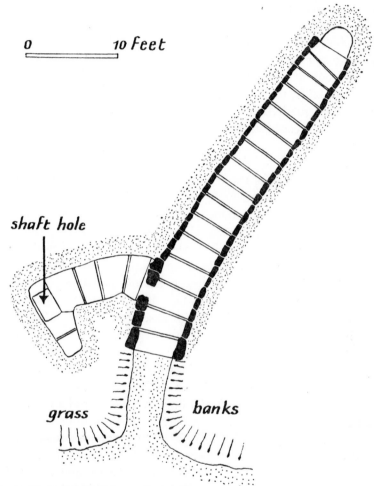

0 _____ 10 feet

shaft hole

grass

banks

Fig 53 Plan of Boleigh fogou, Cornwall

from Pytheas, it should relate to the south-west and could be applicable to the fogous.

It is apparent from finds of Iron Age B pottery at Boscaswell, Boleigh and Treveneague and from others of Roman character at Carn Euny that the fogous are of pre-Roman origin, but as an essential element in the domestic economy of the Penwith settlements, they continued in use during the Roman period. Their limited distribution, which practically coincides with that of the courtyard-house, points to a distinctive group of Celtic people in west Penwith, the ancient Belerion. In all probability, they constituted a *pagus*, and as such, became one of the territorial subdivisions of the *Civitas Dumnoniorum* when the new social order was established.

Sacred Sites

Some sacred places of the Iron Age survived through Roman times: the Celtic term for a sanctuary or grove, *nimet*, was incorporated in *Nemetostatio*, a place mentioned in the Ravenna Cosmography and located at North Tawton (p 164). The element appears in the Doomsday village names in this area and in the Nympton villages near South Molton, in the region where the Rose Ash bowl was found (p 156). Another name in the Cosmography, *Devionissio*, means the place on the holy stream. Although no temples have been discovered, native cult-centres can be inferred at two hill-top sites. At Cadbury hill-fort in the lower Exe valley, there was a shaft 54ft deep from which many bronze bracelets, rings and beads of late Roman date were recovered in 1848. There are the sort of personal things that were customary as votive offerings at shrines, as at Woodeaton in Oxfordshire. At Bosence, St Erth, there was a similar shaft 36ft deep in the corner of a rectangular hill-top enclosure, from which a pewter jug of third to fourth century type and a shallow tin dish were recovered in 1756 with other objects. The dish which has been cut down from a larger vessel has a cursive inscription stating it was dedicated to Mars by Aelius Modestus, and in centre a *Rho* or R in another script. Mars was worshipped as a fertility god as well as a war god by the Celts and the dish was probably used with the jug at a nearby shrine for offerings and libations. Analogous deep shafts or wells were associated with Romano-British temples at Pagan's Hill, Chew Stoke, in Somerset, and at Jordan's Hill, Weymouth, where bird bones from sacrifices were in the filling.

Tin Mining and Industry

The right to mine precious metals was vested in the Emperor in Roman times and the mines were either worked as a state concern, with convict labour under military direction, as at the Dolaucothi gold mine in Wales and in the silver-lead mines on Mendip, or they were leased to private speculators, as in Derbyshire. The profits from mining thus went to the central government and only benefited the canton indirectly, as is apparent from the poverty and backwardness of the south-west.

It is evident that the Romans had advance information about the richness of the argentiferous lead on the Mendips because by AD 49 lead ingots, the by-product of silver, were being stamped with the Emperor Claudius' name. This early success probably prompted an attempt by the military to prospect for metals in mid-Cornwall AD c 60–70 (p 164), but there is no suggestion of large-scale mining. The prospectors would find that the natives directed them only to the tin streams, and since the Romans were well supplied with this metal from northern Spain, it was not profitable to work. The Callington deposits of silver (argentiferous copper) which had been utilised in the Iron Age (p 151) apparently were not worked.

During the second century the tin was worked by the local inhabitants, as at Castle Gotha (p 146) where part of an ingot mould was found. When the Spanish mines were exhausted in the mid-third century, the situation was changed and there was a renewed demand for tin in north-western Europe. In particular with the massive production of *antoniniani*, coins of debased metal with a wash of silver, which replaced the *denarius* in the third century, tin was needed in increasing quantities by new mints like Trier set up by the Gallic Emperor Postumus (AD 258–268). It was apparently the tin streams of mid-Cornwall that were now worked, not those of West Penwith. The 40lb tin ingot from Carnanton, St Mawgan-in-Pyder with a worn imperial inscription of the fourth century shows that metal was smelted under official control. Other late Roman finds from the tin streams are a pewter cup from Halviggan, St Stephen-in-Brannel, a late third-century coin hoard with a tin or pewter dish from Carnon, Devoran, and some oddments from Treloy, St Columb Minor. More signs of government activity are the repair or making of roads in the mining districts of south Cornwall revealed by the milestones of Gordian III (AD 235–240) at Gwennap Pit, of Postumus (AD 258–268) at St Hilary, and of Constantine I (AD 306–308) at Breage and Tintagel.

The increased number of late third- and fourth-century coins found in mid and west Cornwall, shows that mining brought some money into the region, though only in small amounts to the native settlements like Goldherring or Godrevy (p 177). Most of it is found in hoards; like the 1600 found in a pot under a stone near Breage. This phenomenon is not peculiar to Cornwall; the debased *antoniniani* of the Gallic Emperors which make up most of the hoards were repudiated by Aurelian in AD 274 and throughout Britain many savings were then abandoned. The fourth-century hoards, of which six are recorded in Cornwall, are more significant of the prosperity of the region during the Constantinian epoch.

The increased output of Cornish tin in the late third and fourth centuries was also used for the production of tableware, principally pewter jugs and dishes, composed of tin alloyed with lead or copper. As in later times, polished pewter was a good substitute for the silver used by the wealthy. Pewter is known to have been made at St Just-in-Penwith, where two pieces of a stone mould for making dishes were found. The pieces fitted one inside the other and a third mould stone would have enabled two dishes to be cast at the same time. It was also made in Somerset at Lansdown, Bath, and at Camerton, an industrial settlement on the Fossway, where stone moulds for a skillet and an oval dish have been found, and where lead from Mendip was accessible. Vessels with a high tin content are likely to have been made in Cornwall, like the flagon of 96 per cent tin from Carhayes, into which 2,500 *antoniniani* of AD 250–75 were crammed when it was hidden under some stones beside a creek. The distribution along the south coast indicates that the trade was sea-borne; a flagon from Goodrington also with a high tin content was found below the low tide level in Torbay.

Another local industry was salt production for which there is evidence in the Lizard peninsula and in the Somerset levels. At Trebarveth, St Keverne, the method used was evaporation of sea water in coarse earthenware troughs, set over a slow fire burning in a rectangular oven or flue served by a stoke-hole at one end. The salt produced, estimated at some 3lb per firing, probably was packed for transport into pottery jars made locally of characteristic gabbroitic clay. The oven was inside an oval building on the edge of the cliff associated with a field system, showing that the industry was a part-time occupation for the owners: the date was from the second century onwards. In north Somerset there was extensive flooding again in the third century AD, resulting in the deposit of 7ft to 12ft of alluvial clay in the Highbridge area and a shift of the coastline of Bridgwater Bay some eight miles inland. Near Chilton Polden there are mounds of pottery and briquetage (broken bits of the evaporating vessels) indicating not only a salt works but also potteries making black-burnished ware in the third and fourth centuries AD, some of which could have been used as salt containers.

A fine metal-work industry surprisingly flourished on the small island of Nor' Nour in the Scillies during the second century AD. The site was occupied in the Iron Age and the coins show that it continued to be inhabited through the Roman period. The main products were brooches and rings, many with attractive multi-coloured enamel insets, and of designs that are without exact parallels in Britain.

THE FOURTH CENTURY IN EXETER

Historically and archaeologically little is known about the fourth century. The canton probably now belonged to one of the four sub-divisions of the province known as *Britannia Prima*, administered from Cirencester *(Corinium Dobunnorum)* (Fig 48). In *Isca*, very few of the later Roman levels have survived and there are no remains of luxurious town houses of the Constantinian epoch such as have been found in Cirencester or Dorchester. The coin series continues to the reign of Magnus Maximus (AD 383–88) but the Theodosian issues (AD 388–93) apparently never reached the city though they occur in a hoard near Honiton and

in several in north Somerset. The cantonal organisation probably survived in some form into the fifth century: on the south side of the municipal building which replaced the early military baths (p 166) two rooms
were added, built in roughly coursed stone partly cemented with clay:
finds of imported *amphorae* (Fig 56), to be discussed in Chapter IX,
show they continued to be used in the fifth and sixth centuries. One
Roman town house near St Pancras church had a crudely constructed
stone hypocaust inserted into a room that was a fourth-century addition
to the main block: here too imported pottery suggested occupation continuing into the fifth century. Elsewhere there is evidence of decay: the
gravel surface of the Forum was covered with 6ins of fine black mould
and two rubbish pits had been dug in it containing coins of AD 370–80.
It is evident that when the Emperor Honorious wrote to the Cities
(civitates) of Britain in AD 410 telling them that henceforth they must
fend for themselves, the mechanism of the *Civitas Dumnoniorum* was
running down.

SUMMARY

The prosperity of the Dumnonii in Roman times thus was a fitful affair.
For the majority the change of rulers affected their way of life very little;
they were freed from the demands of their chieftains for labour at fortifications but they had to satisfy those of the tax collectors. So far as the
limited evidence goes, provided by fields and fogous, mixed farming
remained the basis of their economy: its small scale militated against
an increase in population.

The canton as a whole was backward and resistant to change; it was
the courtyard house that became the mode in west Cornwall, not the
Roman one at Magor. Only at *Isca*, the cantonal town and in east Devon
was there any real change in building style and way of life. The prosperity that the revival of tin mining brought in the third and four centuries was slight and limited by official control. To realise what the
Dumnonii missed, we have only to look at the development of the many
country houses, like Low Ham and Frampton with their new mosaics, in
the adjoining canton of the Durotriges during the early fourth century.

CHAPTER IX

Early Christian Period to AD 600

In AD 410 Honorius Emperor of the West wrote to the *civitates* of Britain to tell them, in answer to an appeal for military aid, that henceforth they must fend for themselves; each canton now had to rely on its own resources. In eastern England this sub-Roman epoch of independence was brief, lasting only till the influx of Anglo-Saxon settlers from AD 450 onwards. In the south-west, as in Wales, it was prolonged, lasting in Devon and west Somerset until the end of the seventh century when the west Saxon king Centwine 'drove the Britons as far as the sea' (AD 682) and in Cornwall until the ninth or tenth century when first King Egbert (AD 823–39) and finally King Athelstan (AD 924–39) overcame Celtic resistance. Here the Celtic society that developed in consequence of the end of Roman rule will be briefly examined as far as the limited archaeological material permits, and we shall take leave of Dumnonia before the beginning of the Saxon attacks.

MEMORIAL STONES

The principal source of information is still the memorial stones; the earliest consist of an undecorated slab or pillar on which has been cut in Roman capitals the name of an individual, his parentage and the Latin formula *hic iacit*, he lies here, or *hic in tumulo iacit*, he lies here in the grave, or occasionally *Memoria*, the memorial of; the preceding name is usually in the genitive case. Memorials of the late sixth or early seventh century can be distinguished by the increasing number of letters in cursive or half-uncial script that derive from contemporary Gallic

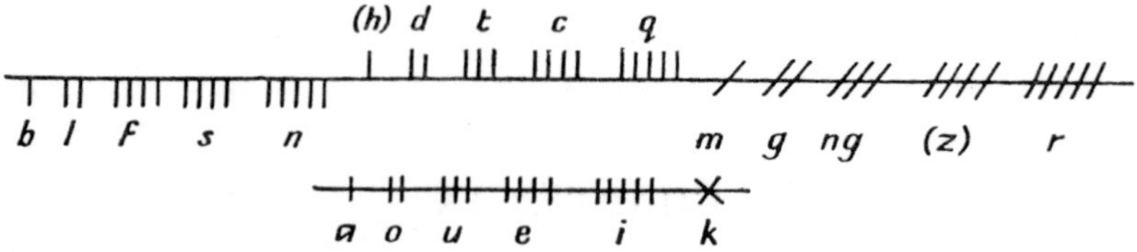

Fig 54 The Ogam alphabet

epigraphy. Despite the formulae, it is rare to find a grave below the stone; the best authenticated is at Hayle, where the fifth century memorial of CVNAIDE was found in 1843 beside a grave containing ashes and charcoal, which was covered by loose stones.

The inscriptions show that the memorials are related to Roman tombstones and reflect the Roman social order. Cunaide's epitaph records that she lived for thirty-three years and is aligned horizontally in the Roman manner. The names of the people commemorated are often recognisably Roman, like IVSTVS at St Kew, LATINVS at Worthyvale or of Roman descent like the Celtic VLCAGNVS son of SEVERVS from Nanscowe, and CAVVDVS son of CIVILIS from Lynton. At Buckland Monachorum, DOBVNNVS son of ENABARRVS is described as a smith *(faber)*, at Rialton another person as child of a tribune, presumably a late Roman official, whilst on the worn stone on Sourton Down, Okehampton, AVDETVS is termed *Princeps*. This title was used by some barbarian rulers in imperial times, but also by Frankish and Burgundian kings in the sixth century.

It is evident that Latin retained its prestige along with the Roman tradition, even if the masons were unsure of their declensions and spelling. Nevertheless it is the Celtic names that predominate roughly three to one and it is not uncommon for two generations to have Celtic names like DVNOCATVS the son of MERCAGNVS at Lancarffe. The name is lost of the man who was grandson *(Nepos)* of CARATACVS, a famous name in early Celtic history, on the memorial which stands on Winsford Hill in west Somerset. Women too were occasionally commemorated like NONNITA on the Tregoney stone or CVNAIDE at Hayle.

The Celtic population included some Irish settlers, Goidels or Q

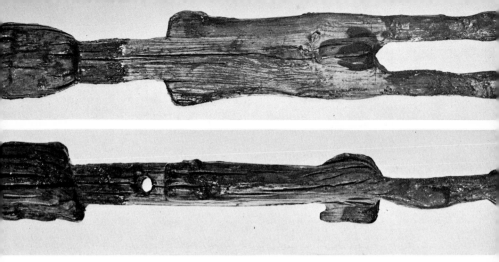

21a (*left*)
Bronze tripod
mount, with
Achilles riding
Cheiron the
centaur, from
Sidmouth,
Devon.
Height 7in.
Exeter
Museum

21b (*right*)
Wooden idols,
oak, from
Teigngrace,
Newton Abbot,
Devon.
Height 13·3in.
Watts Blake
and Bearne

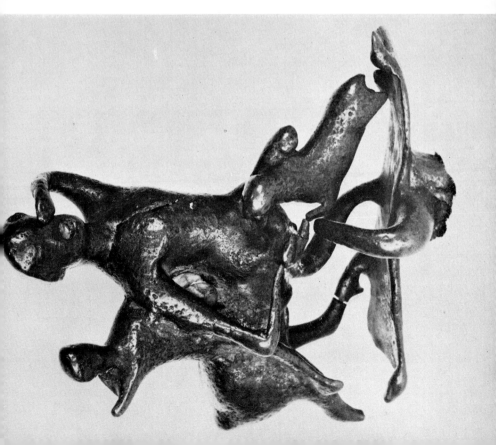

22 The Roman city wall, inner by-pass, Exeter

23a *(above)* Romano-British settlement at Chysauster, Gulval, West Cornwall 23b *(below)* Fogou at Carn Euny, Romano-British settlement, Sancreed, West Cornwall

24a *(left)* Early Christian memorial stone from Fardel, Ivybridge, South Devon. Height 5ft 6in. British Museum 24b *(below)* Tintagel Celtic monastery, Cornwall

Celts: this is shown by their names and lineage cut in Ogams along the edges of their memorial stones. The Ogam stroke alphabet (Fig 54) was developed in southern Ireland in the late third or fourth century AD; the twenty letters consist of combinations of one to five strokes cut at varying angles on either side of the arris or edge of the stone. Normally the Ogams render either the same name as the Latin, as on the stone of VLCAGNVS, or its Celtic equivalent as *Igenavi* for INGENVI (Ingenuus) both on stones at Lewannick. On the Fardel stone, Ivybridge (Plate 24) the Celtic word *Maqvi* (Mac, son of), is used in the original Ogams, SVAQQVCI MAQI QICI, both Irish names and in the secondary Latin inscription of FANONVS MAQVI RINI; a third name, SAGRANVS, was added in the early seventh century. The stone thus commemorated three people of Irish descent.

The memorials in general are those of local rulers and dynasties, and indicate that Celtic society had reverted to the aristocratic pattern of the Iron Age. PRINCEPS AVDETVS has already been mentioned; CVMREGNVS at Southhill embodies a royal title as does TIGERNVS on Lundy. RIALO-BRANVS on the Men Scryfys pillar at Madron means 'Royal Raven' whilst CVNOMORVS, whose son DRVSTAVS' memorial was set up on the ridgeway near Castle Dore, Fowey, has been plausibly identified with the *Marcus dictus Quonomorus*, mentioned in the ninth-century life of St Paul Aurelian, and with the King Mark of the Tristan legend. From such local rulers emerged the kings or overlords of historic times, including the tyrant Constantine whom Gildas in the mid sixth century named with such vituperation and King Geraint who fought with Ine of Wessex in AD 710.

These rulers were nominally Christian: this is evident from the formulae and from the occasional carving of the Chi-Rho, a monogram formed out of the Greek initial letters of Christ (XP), such as can be seen on the memorial of SENILVS at St Just in Penwith or of BROCAGNVS at St Endellion. The Christian symbols *Alpha* and *Omega* also were used. The faith was introduced into the south-west in the fourth century as throughout the Empire generally; there were poor Christians in Exeter who used a black cooking-pot marked with a Chi-Rho. The monogram on the stones, however, with the crooklike *Rho* is a Gallic form and from this and other epigraphic evidence it appears that Celtic Christianity was nurtured by contact with western and southern Gaul after the breakdown of Roman control in Britain.

The distribution of the stones (Fig 55) is predominantly in the western half of the peninsula with two on Exmoor: none has been found in east Devon. The Ogam stones indicate fifth-century Irish settlements in south-west Devon and in north Cornwall, perhaps of peoples coming from settlements in South Wales where an invasion by the Deisi, a tribe from Waterford, is known to have taken place in late Roman times and where memorials in Ogam are frequent, and several of the same Irish names are found. It was customary to set up the stones in isolation, often on the roadside in the Roman manner, not in churches or churchyards to which many have been moved in recent times. The ancient route across the peninsula from Padstow to Fowey has three

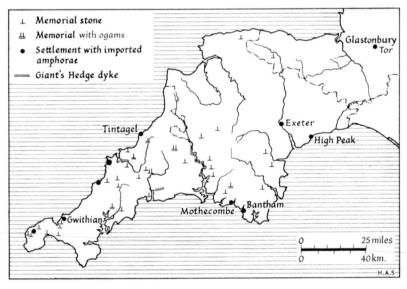

Fig 55 Distribution of memorial stones and imported pottery of the V–VII centuries AD

stones sited on it, including the Castle Dore stone, and the stones on Winsford Hill and Sourton Down are both on ridgeways: similar isolated roadside siting occurs in South Wales. It was, however, by the seaways that Dumnonia maintained contact with the surviving Roman and Celtic civilisation in Gaul and the Mediterranean.

POTTERY AND THE WINE TRADE

Until very recently nothing was known of the places where these people named on the stones lived: their recognition began with the discovery in 1940 at a hill-fort at Garranes in southern Ireland of sherds of foreign wine jugs and amphorae in association with Irish metalwork of sixth-century date. In the south-west similar wares had previously been recorded from the early monastic site at Tintagel (p 199) and later were recovered from small settlements at Bantham, south Devon, and Gwithian, west Cornwall. Recent excavations, however, have demonstrated that the principal recipients were the native princes in their refurbished hill-forts as at South Cadbury and Cadbury, Congresbury in Somerset, High Peak in Devon, or Dinas Powys in South Wales. In all some twenty sites are now known in the south-west and South Wales, including the Roman towns of Exeter and Ilchester. Four main varieties of pottery were imported, all wheel-made: first fine little red bowls and dishes, some with a cross or other motif impressed on the interior (Class A); secondly, combed or corrugated amphorae (Fig 56), thin-walled vessels in cream, buff or orange ware (Class B), which form the bulk of the sherds from the south-west; thirdly, mortaria bowls in a grey fabric with a blue-black surface (Class D); and fourthly, cooking pots, jugs, bowls and small beakers in hard grey ware (Class E). The first two groups originated in the eastern Mediterranean in the late fourth and fifth centuries, parallels having been found as far away as Antioch and Constantinople with others distributed in the western Mediterranean: the grey wares (D and E) are held to come from western Gaul, probably from the Bordeaux region. At Gwithian the stratigraphical evidence indicates that A and B were the earliest imports dating from the fifth and sixth centuries and that E came later, in the sixth and seventh centuries.

The trade route from the Mediterranean was through the straits of Gibraltar, and up the Atlantic coast. The preponderance of amphorae and jugs shows that the merchant-venturers were carrying wine and, judging by the occasional residue, olive oil, which was needed for lighting as well as for cooking. Some fine glass and beads from Egypt were sometimes included in the cargo and also from the Merovingian factories at Cologne, all tempting luxuries for British princes. The landing places were at the mouth of rivers like Bantham on the Avon or Mothecombe on the Erme where there are sheltered anchorages, sandy shores where a boat could be beached, and ridgeways to the hinterland. Remains of fires, piles of shells and animal bones found with the potsherds in black layers under the dunes are all that remain of the encampments of the merchants or their customers. It may be supposed that the boats made the return journey loaded with a profitable cargo; there is the well-known story in the life of John the Almsgiver, patriarch of Alexandria (AD 611–619), of the merchant ship sailing from Egypt to Britain with corn which relieved a famine and returning with a cargo of tin.

Fig 56 Imported amphorae, Class B

SETTLEMENTS

At Gwithian a permanent native settlement of this period has been located to the south of the Bronze Age site (p 105) on the edge of an old tidal creek. It began in the fifth century as a single family hut, with the inhabitants using hand-made dishes and jars, homely copies of Romano-British originals, and acquiring some amphorae of imported wine. During the sixth century the hut was replaced by three others each about 10–12ft in diameter, with turf walls on a stone foundation. Rubbish from both periods was deposited in pits or on a midden, and shows that a lot of shellfish were eaten as well as beef, mutton and pork: bird and fish bones were strewn on the hut floors. Iron was worked and small fields were cultivated on the sandy soil. The pottery now used included coarse, straight-sided pots, with nicked or fingered rims and on the base impressions of chopped grass or straw, on which the pots had been stood to dry before firing. This device was to prevent the clay sticking to its resting place and was used in Cornwall until the eleventh century; similar grass-marked pottery occurs in northern Ireland where it has been found in souterrains and settlements of the Early Christian period. Sherds of imported amphorae and of wheel-made cooking pots were associated with the grass-marked wares at Gwithian, showing that this modest homestead participated in the trade overseas. The same applies to Porthmeor (p 177) where occupation continued from Roman times.

Moving up the social scale there is evidence that some hill-forts were re-occupied. At High Peak, Sidmouth, a fort which has been heavily eroded, a thick layer of rubbish containing imported amphorae had been thrown on to the inner rampart and into the ditch: a radio-carbon date of AD 489 showed that the defences were in existence in the late fifth century. Since no Iron Age material has been found here, it could be that this coastal hill-fort was a sub-Roman construction. At Chun, west Cornwall, a grass-marked pot and an amphora sherd have been recognised from one of the radial compartments built against the inner face of the massive stone wall of this small circular fort situated on a hill-top in the Land's End peninsula. Tin smelting was carried on in another compartment nearby. Trevelgue promontory fort, Newquay (Plate 18a), apparently continued to be occupied since amphora sherds are known to exist in the unpublished material. At Castle Dore hill-fort (p 142) near Fowey, there is a series of stone-packed postholes belonging to rectangular buildings which were stratigraphically later than those of the Iron Age round huts. The excavator, Ralegh Radford, considered that these belonged to a large aisled hall, 90ft by 40ft, with a central ridge support, a porch, and a square kitchen annex, with a subsidiary hall, 65ft by 25ft, nearby. The evidence has recently been republished by Philip Rahtz. No imported amphorae were found here and the post-Roman date depends archaeologically on a yellow bead which is not closely dateable and two rim sherds of a jar and bowl of wheel-made grey pottery. The ascription to the sixth century gains some support from the nearby memorial of Drustaus, son of Cunomorus (p 189) and from place-names which point to this area as the scene of the King Mark and Tristan story.

In Somerset, in former Durotrigian territory adjoining the Dumnonii, refortification on a larger scale is in evidence; at Cadbury Congresbury, where excavations are still in progress, an 8½ acre Iron Age hill-fort was altered and a variety of new dwellings erected; at South Cadbury the whole circuit of the 18 acre fort was elaborately refortified with a timber-framed stone-faced rampart and new gates: a timber aisled hall, 63ft by 34ft, not dissimilar to that at Castle Dore, was erected on the hill-top. The excavator, Leslie Alcock, considers that the site was a focus of military resistance to the Saxons pushing westwards in the sixth century. It is clear that some Celtic rulers lived in some state on fortified hill-tops, reverting to the pattern of society in the early Iron Age.

It is now apparent from stratified finds of imported amphorae (Fig 56) that some corporate life persisted in Exeter in the fifth and sixth centuries. In the centre of the city a spacious room with an ante-chamber was built on to the municipal offices, which had replaced the military baths on the founding of the cantonal capital (p 166). The masonry was crude, using rubble and clay with a poor soluble mortar for the facing joints. Whether this building remained in use until the

Saxons took control of the city in the late seventh century, or whether it was used for secular or ecclesiastical purposes in connection with a bishopric, is quite uncertain, as is the relationship of the city dwellers to the native princes.

BURIALS

The mode of burial from late Roman times onwards was an extended inhumation with the head laid to the west so that the Christian might rise up facing east on the Day of Judgement. Roman cemeteries were sited by law outside the towns or settlements and might contain family plots with stone-built mausolea and space round them for burials of their dependents, as is now evident from the recent excavation of the Poundbury cemetery at Dorchester. Some continuation of these Roman customs is apparent at the large sub-Roman cemetery at Cannington near Bridgwater, excavated by Philip Rahtz. Some 350 graves were excavated in 1962–3, but many more were quarried away in the nineteenth century. There were two tombs indicating the burial places of distinguished individuals, one a grave on the hill-top surrounded by polygonal walling and a rock-cut ditch, probably the remains of a mausoleum, the other the grave of a young girl under a mound approached by a worn path in the limestone rock. The very scanty finds indicated that the cemetery was used from the late fourth till the eighth century. The most likely site for the settlement was the nearby hill-fort, Cannington Camp, from which late Roman material has been recovered. In the absence of grave-goods it is impossible to date cemeteries of extended and orientated burials in the Christian manner, such as those found at Trevone, Padstow, in slate-lined graves which post-dated burials of early Roman date, or isolated graves such as that of a woman uncovered by road works at Woodleigh in the South Hams.

There is no record as yet of an inscribed memorial stone being found *in situ* in an early cemetery in the south-west, or in South Wales, though the discoveries of three stones on Lundy in a graveyard are suggestive. Outside this area, the best recorded example is the Catstane, the memorial of VETTA, daughter of VICTVS at Kirkliston, near the Firth of Forth, which was erected on a small mound at the edge of a cemetery of fifty-one graves in the sixth century.

Although urban-based Christianity started in Dumnonia in late Roman times, its spread to the Celtic population generally in the sixth century was due to missionary monks coming from other Celtic lands, principally from South Wales but also from Ireland and Brittany. This is known because unlike the English custom whereby new churches were dedicated to an appropriate apostle like St Peter, the Celtic churches took the name of their founder who had converted the district and often settled there on land granted by the local ruler. In Cornwall alone, 174 out of the 212 ancient parishes are dedicated to a western saint and about 50 in Devon. By a critical study of the dedications combined with the written lives, which survive mostly in medieval manuscripts and incorporate a number of obvious inventions, some idea of the conversion can be obtained.

The initial impulse came from South Wales: at Llantwit Major, Glamorgan, St Iltyd had founded a monastery and a school of learning in the late fifth century from which a succession of powerful personalities crossed the Bristol Channel to evangelise in the peninsula. In the first life of St Samson (c AD 480–560), written at his Breton foundation at Dol as early as the seventh century, there are details of the Welsh saint landing near Padstow, encountering monks from a previous mission at St Kew *(Docco)* and travelling overland with a waggon loaded with sacred books and holy vessels. In the nearby district called *Tricurium* (now Trigg Major) he saw the pagan people dancing and worshipping a stone idol and a young man racing on a horse with their chief *(comes)* watching the ceremony, a fascinating survival of rites from prehistoric times: it is alleged that the saint cut a cross on the standing stone after remonstrating with them. At the end of his mission, Samson re-embarked probably from Fowey for Dol in Brittany. Cornwall had also been a halfway house for St Paul Aurelian, who was born in Glamorgan, studied at Llantwit and came by the same trans-peninsular route to

King Mark Cunomorus before proceeding to Ushant and Saint Pol de-Léon. St Petroc, a contemporary of Samson, remained in Cornwall, founding his first monastery near Padstow and later moved to Bodmin to land given by the local rulers *(reguli)*, Theodorus and Constantine, in the mid sixth century. Other dedications attest missions by those of Welsh descent to mid and east Cornwall and north Devon, whilst the Irish, like St Breaca of Breage or St Hya who gives her name to St Ives, were principally concerned with west Cornwall. There are also dedications to saints from Brittany, like St Winwaloe of Landévennec at Gunwalloe, St Corentin of Quimper at Cury in the Lizard whilst relics of St Rumon (Ronan of Locronan) were translated from Ruan Lanihorne on the Fal to Tavistock in the twelfth century, although no record has survived in the literature of missions by these saints to Britain.

The settlements of the saints were primitive, consisting of a little church or oratory, and cells for the individual monks which were merely huts, such as St Paul Aurelian is recorded to have built beside a spring on Ushant or such as survive on the islands off the west coast of Ireland. There was a strong desire in the Celtic Church to withdraw from the world to the wild places, just as the Theban monks of Egypt had withdrawn to the desert, following the example of saints Paul and Antony in the fourth century. This is well exemplified by the site chosen for the early monastery at Tintagel (Plate 24b) on an exposed cliff-ringed promontory, now practically an island, 250ft sheer above the Atlantic. The monks lived in small contiguous rectangular cells, poorly built of stones and clay, with beaten earth floors and thatched roofs. The main complex clusters round the Norman chapel, which probably has replaced an original wooden church, and the graveyard containing the founder's tomb, or *leacht*, a masonry foundation five feet square. There are other groups of cells on a shelf on the east side of the headland as well as a long narrow building with internal seating identified as the *scriptorium*. There is also a little chamber with a burnt paved floor which was probably a sweat house, in which water was thrown on heated stones to provide a vapour bath. On the northern cliff-edge there was a corn-drying kiln, evidence of inland cultivation. The monastery was founded in the early sixth century, probably by St Julian or Juliot, one of the children of Brychan, from South Wales and there were three or four building periods before it was deserted in the ninth century. There were cells for about thirty monks. Their life must have been harsh and poverty-stricken in this wild setting: nevertheless they obtained amphorae of wine and oil, needed for the services, from the foreign merchants.

The hermitage on St Helen's in the Isles of Scilly occupied a site similarly withdrawn from the world and exposed to the elements. Although the only relics found during excavation were of medieval date the layout is that of a Celtic foundation, beginning with a round hut and a rectangular stone oratory ascribed to the founder St Elidius, to which three rectangular cells and a later chapel were added, all enclosed by a precinct wall.

In contrast to Tintagel, the majority of Celtic churches are on sheltered sites and in touch with the local population. St Petroc's monastery at Bodmin was at the head of a valley which winds down to the wooded gorge of the Camel and was situated on fertile land occupied in the Iron Age from the evidence of the nearby Canyke hill-fort. At Gunwalloe in the Lizard, St Winwaloe's church, now isolated beside the cove, is close to a cliff-castle; later grass-marked and bar-lug pottery found a short distance away is evidence of continuity of settlement, as is the manor farm of Winnianton, which gave its name to the Hundred in late Saxon times. Other sites favoured are the ends of spurs as at Petrockstow, but the high ground was avoided; wooded valleys were sometimes chosen for a hermitage as at Landkey, and clearing thus initiated. The early churches have not survived. Most were likely to have been timber constructions, rebuilt in stone from the eighth or ninth centuries onwards. The first church at Glastonbury, the *Vetusta Ecclesia*, is known from William of Malmesbury's account to have been a wooden structure with wattlework, 60ft long by 26ft wide; it was standing when King Ine of Wessex built his stone church in the Kentish style to the east of it c AD 700, and remained until destroyed by fire in AD 1184. The little oratory of St Perran, now wrecked and isolated in the dunes behind

Perranporth, probably retains its original form and incorporates some pre-Norman masonry.

SUMMARY

These glimpses of Dumnonia in the fifth and sixth centuries show a land peopled and ruled by Celts, mainly of Romano-British descent and proud of their lineage and limited knowledge of Latin. There were also others newly arrived from Ireland and South Wales who spoke Goidelic and introduced the Ogam script. So far as the available evidence goes, their mode of life differed little from that in the Iron Age. Contact with the outside world was by the western seaways, with traders from the Mediterranean, reminiscent of early Bronze Age times, and with compatriots in Wales, Ireland and Brittany, all places linked culturally with the peninsula in megalithic and Iron Age times. The motive that impelled the people across the sea was no longer a search for land to settle but the desire to spread the Christian gospel. With Brittany the link was especially strong. Britons from southern England had migrated there in the face of the Saxon invasions after AD 450 and others from the West Country, including east Devon, must have followed with the West Saxon advance to the Cotswolds in AD 567. By the mid-sixth century there were so many that the peninsula was referred to by Gregory of Tours as Britannia instead of by its Roman name of Armorica. Another sign of the migration is that the Breton and Cornish languages remained closely akin.

Although the south-west was never wholly depopulated, the political cohesion gained during four centuries of Roman rule was lost; as we have seen, the Dark Ages was an era of petty kings and independent local dynasties, of individual saints and independent monasteries. Therefore, when the time came, Dumnonia was ill-equipped to offer effective resistance to the West Saxons.

Field Monuments to Visit

A representative selection has been made from those which are not too difficult of access and which are well preserved. Sites are arranged topographically, in chronological order. Those marked * are in charge of the Dept of the Environment, Ancient Monuments' Branch, + of the National Trust. Permission should be asked of the owner before visiting others on private property.

West Cornwall

+	Lanyon Quoit, Madron, chamber tomb	sw 430337
	Zennor Quoit, chamber tomb	sw 469380
*	Carn Gluze, St Just, Entrance Grave	sw 353315
	Pennance, Zennor, Entrance Grave	sw 448376
	Merry Maidens stone circle and the	sw 433245
	Pipers standing stones, Rosmodres	sw 434248
	Carn Brea, Camborne, hill-fort	sw 685408
	Chun Castle, Morvah, hill-fort	sw 405339
+	Treryn Dinas, St Levan, promontory fort	sw 398220
+	Trencrom, Lelant, hill-fort	sw 518362
*	Chysauster, Gulval, native village	sw 473350
*	Carn Euny, Sancreed, native village and fogou	sw 402289
	Men Scryfys, Madron, memorial stone	sw 427353

For other monuments, see *Antiquities of the Land's End district*, West Cornwall Field Club Guide No. 2.

East Cornwall

	Pawton, St Breocke, chamber tomb	sw 966697
*	Trethevy, St Cleer, chamber tomb	sx 259689
	Castilly, Lanivet, henge	sx 031629
*	The Hurlers, Linkinhorne, stone circles	sx 258714
	Rillaton, Linkinhorne, barrow	sx 260719
	Taphouse, Braddock, barrows	sx 146633
		175632
	Harlyn Bay, St Merryn, cemetery	sw 878754
	Castle-an-Dinas, St Columb, hill-fort	sw 945625
	Hall Rings, Pelynt, multiple enclosure fort	sx 214555
	The Rumps, Polzeath, promontory fort	sw 935810
	Trevelgue, Newquay, promontory fort	sw 825630
	Castle Dore, Golant, hill-fort	sx 103548
*	Tintagel, Celtic monastery	ss 050890
	Lewannick church, Ogam memorial stones	sx 275808

For other monuments see *Antiquities of the Newquay–Padstow district* West Cornwall Field Club Guide No. 7.

Dartmoor and South Devon

	Corringdon Ball, South Brent, chamber tomb	sx 670613
	Scorhill, Gidleigh, stone circle	sx 655873
	Shoveldown, Chagford, stone rows	sx 650860
	Merrivale stone rows and circle	sx 534748
	Grimspound, Manaton, enclosed settlement	sx 700809
	Kestor, Chagford, huts and fields	sx 665867
	Trowlesworthy Warren, enclosed settlements	sx 574645
	Butterdon Hill, Harford, cairns and stone row	sx 660587

For other Dartmoor sites, see *Dartmoor National Park Guide.*

	Farway barrows	st 151960
	Hembury, Honiton, hill-fort	st 101030
	Milber Down, Newton Abbot, multiple-enclosure fort	sx 885698
	Prestonbury, Drewsteignton, multiple-enclosure fort	sx 746900
+	Bolt Tail promontory fort	sx 670397

Exeter, Roman city wall, Southernhay and Northernhay Gardens.
Tavistock, memorial stones in the vicarage garden.   SX 480744

North Devon and West Somerset
    Five Barrows, Exmoor   SS 732368
    Chapman barrows, Parracombe   SS 695435
    Clovelly Dykes, multiple-enclosure fort   SS 311235
    Countisbury promontory fort   SS 741995
    Old Burrow, Countisbury, Roman fortlet   SS 788495
+   Winsford Hill, memorial stone   SS 890335
    For other Exmoor sites see *Exmoor National Park Guide.*

Museums

Cornwall
Truro The Royal Institution of Cornwall's museum: a well-arranged collection from the county, including finds from excavations at Knackyboy, Scilly, Crig-a-Minnis barrow, St Mawgan-in-Pyder hill-fort, The Rumps, Carvossa, Nanstallon Roman fort, and Tintagel Celtic monastery.
Penzance Penlee House: a small collection of Cornish Bronze Age pottery.
Harlyn Bay near Padstow: finds from the Iron Age cemetery.

Devon
Exeter Rougemont House museum: finds from Hembury neolithic settlement and hill-fort, Farway and Upton Pyne barrows, Kestor and Dean Moor Dartmoor settlements: Roman remains from Exeter and Holcombe villa; replica of Holcombe Iron Age mirror.
Plymouth The City Museum and Art Gallery: Bronze Age pottery from Dartmoor settlements; finds from Mount Batten.
Torquay The Torquay Natural History Society's museum: finds from excavations at Hazard Hill neolithic settlement, Milber Down hill-fort and Bantham early Christian settlement.

Somerset
Taunton The County Museum at Taunton Castle contains a well-arranged collection from Somerset including the Wick barrow, Bronze

Age ornament hoards, the Shapwick boat, Meare Lake village and the Low Ham mosaic.

Glastonbury (summer only). Lake village material.

London The British Museum (Dept of Prehistory and Roman Britain): the Rillaton cup, Morvah and Towednack gold hoards, Rose Ash bowl, Trenoweth collar, Polden Hill hoard, Holcombe mirror, Fardel memorial stone.

Bristol The City Museum: the Wraxall torc.

Cambridge Museum of Archaeology and Ethnology: the god-dolly and other Neolithic finds from the Somerset levels.

Oxford The Ashmolean Museum: the Crediton hoard, Bosence Roman pewter.

Bibliography

ABBREVIATIONS

Ant J	*The Antiquaries Journal*
Arch J	*The Archaeological Journal*
Arch	*Archaeologia*
CA	*Cornish Archaeology*
Inst of Arch	*Institute of Archaeology, London University*
J Brit Arch Ass	*Journal of the British Archaeological Association*
JRS	*Journal of Roman Studies*
JRIC	*Journal of the Royal Institute of Cornwall*
Med Arch	*Journal of Medieval Archaeology*
Num Chron	*Numismatic Chronicle*
PDAES, PDAS	*Proceedings of the Devon Archaeological (Exploration) Society*
PPS	*Proceedings of the Prehistoric Society*
P Som AS	*Proceedings of the Somerset Archaeological and Natural History Society*
PWCFC	*Proceedings of the West Cornwall Field Club*
TDA	*Transactions of the Devonshire Association*

GENERAL WORKS

Borlase, W. C., *Naenia Cornubiae* (1872)
Dobson, D. P., *Archaeology of Somerset* (1931)
Grinsell, L. V., *The Archaeology of Exmoor* (1970)
Hencken, H. O'N., *Archaeology of Cornwall and Scilly* (1932)

Russell, V., *West Penwith Survey* (1971)

Worth, R. H., *Dartmoor* (1953)

Victoria County History, *Cornwall, Devon, and Somerset* (1906–24). Articles, of varying merit, on Early Man, Stone circles, Ancient earthworks, Romano-British remains, Early Christian monuments

Arch J CXIV (1957) Exeter meeting p126 *et seq*

British Association Handbook, *Exeter and its Region* (1969)

CHAPTER I

Clayden, A. W., *The History of Devonshire Scenery* (1906)

Dewey, H., *British Regional Geology, South-West England* 2nd edition (1948)

Dines, H. G., *The Metaliferous Mining Region of South-West England* (1956)

North, F. J., *The Evolution of the Bristol Channel* (1929)

Simmons, I. G., 'Environment and Early Man on Dartmoor', *PPS* (1969) p203

Welch, F. B. and Kellaway, G. A., *British Regional Geology, Bristol and Gloucester district* (1948)

CHAPTER II

Clark, J. G. D., 'Neolithic bows from Somerset', *PPS* (1963) p50

Coles, J. M. and Hibbert, F. A., 'A Neolithic wooden mallet from the Somerset levels', *Antiquity* (1972)

Coles, J. M., Hibbert, F. A. and Clements, C. F., 'Prehistoric roads and tracks in Somerset', *PPS* (1968) p238; (1970) p125

Fox, A., 'The Castlewitch Ringwork', *Ant J* XXXII (1952) p67

Godwin, H., 'Prehistoric trackways of the Somerset levels', *PPS* (1960) p1; (1963) p17

Grieg, O. and Rankine, W. F., 'A Stone Age settlement system near East Week', *PDAES* V (1953) p8

Houlder, C. H., 'A Neolithic settlement on Hazard Hill, Totnes', *PDAES* no 21 (1963) p2

Liddell, D. M., 'Excavations at Hembury Fort, Devon', 4 reports, 1930,

1931, 1932, 1934–5, *PDAES* I, pp40, 90, 162; II, p135. Details of the Neolithic occupation will be found principally in the third and fourth reports, the pottery in the second and fourth reports. See also, Smith, I. F., 'Causewayed Enclosures'. 'Radio-carbon dates', Fox, A., *Antiquity* (1963) p228

Megaw, J. V. S., 'The Neolithic period in Cornwall', *PWCFC* II (1957–8) p13

Mercer, R., 'The Neolithic settlement on Carn Brea: interim report' *CA* 9 (1970) p53

Peacock, D., 'Neolithic pottery production in Cornwall', *Antiquity* (1969) p145

Piggott, S., *Neolithic Cultures of the British Isles* (1954) Ch2 & 3. Standard text-book for this period

Pollard, S. M., 'Neolithic and Dark Age settlements on High Peak, Sidmouth', *PDAS* 23 (1965) p35. Radio-carbon dates, 25 (1967) p43

Savory, H. N., 'A Neolithic stone axe and wooden handle from Port Talbot, Glam', *Ant J* LI (1971) p296

Smith, I. F., 'Causewayed Enclosures', *Economy and Settlement in Neolithic Britain*, ed Simpson, D. (1971) p89

Smith, I. F., 'Note on the distribution of Neolithic storage pits', *PPS* (1964) p367

Stone, J. F. S. and Wallis, F. S., 'The petrological determination of stone axes', 1st Report, *PPS* (1941) p 50; 2nd Report, *PPS* (1947) p47; 3rd Report, *PPS* (1951) p99

   Evens, E. D., Grinsell, L. V., Piggott, S. and Wallis, F. S., 4th Report, *PPS* (1962) p209

   Evens, E. D., Smith, I.F., Wallis, F. S.,5th Report, *PPS* (1972) p235

Thomas, A. C., 'Carn Brea finds in Camborne Public Library', *C.A.* I. (1962) p104. See also Patchett, F. M., *Arch J* CI (1944) p20 for other pottery from this site.

Thomas, A. C., 'The henge at Castilly, Lanivet', *CA* 3 (1964) p3

Willock, E. H., 'A Neolithic site on Haldon', *PDAES* II (1936) p244. A further note on Haldon, *ibid* III (1937) p33

Woods, G. MacAlpine, 'A Stone Age site in East Devon (Beer Head)', *PDAES* I (1929) p10

CHAPTER III

Ashbee, P., 'Chambered tombs on St Mary's, Scilly', *CA* 2 (1963) p9
Borlase, W. C., 'Typical specimens of Cornish barrows', *Arch* XLIX (1886) p181. Includes Entrance Graves at Tregaseal, Chapel Carn Brea and Carn Gluze (Ballowal). See also *Naenia Cornubiae*
Daniel, Glyn E., *The Prehistoric Chamber-tombs in England and Wales* (1950). South-western tombs are listed on p236–50
Hencken, H. O'N., *The Archaeology of Cornwall and Scilly* (1932) Ch2, Great stone monuments
O'Neil, B. St J., 'The excavation of Knackyboy cairn, St Martin's, Scilly', *Ant* J XXXII (1952) p21
Radford, C. A. R., 'The chambered tomb at Broadsands, Paignton', *PDAES* V (1957–8) p 147
Thomas, A. C. and Wailes, B., 'Sperris Quoit excavation', *CA* 6 (1967) p9

CHAPTER IV

Ashbee, P. 'The excavation of Tregulland Barrow, Treneglos', *Ant J* XXXVIII (1958) p174
Brailsford, J., 'Bronze Age stone monuments of Dartmoor', *Antiquity* (1938) p444. Contains plans of stone rows
Clarke, D. L., *Beaker pottery of Great Britain and Ireland*, 2 vols (1970). The new standard work of classification
Dartmoor Exploration Committee, 'Exploration of barrows and stone circle at Fernworthy', *TDA* XXX (1898) p107
Dudley, D. and Patchett, F. M., 'Excavations on Kerrow farm, Zennor: the long-stone site', *PWCFC* I (1953–4) p44
Eogan, G., 'The excavation of a stone alignment and circle at Cholwich-town, Lee Moor', *PPS* (1964) p25
Giot, P. R., *Brittany* (1960). Contains the most accessible account of comparable Breton monuments

Gray, H. St G., 'Report on the Wick barrow excavations, Stoguersey', *P Som AS* LIV (1908) p1

Gray, H. St G., 'The Stone Circles of East Cornwall', *Arch* LXI (1909) p1

Miles, H. and T. J., 'Excavations on Longstone Downs, St Stephen in Brannel', *CA* 10 (1971) p5

Piggott, S., 'Abercromby and after', *Culture and Environment*, essays presented to Sir Cyril Fox, edited I. Foster and L. Alcock (1963) p53: Useful account of the Beaker peoples

Pollard, S. H., Seven prehistoric sites near Honiton.
   (a) 'Beaker flint-ring on Burnt Common', *PDAS* 25 (1967) p 20
   (b) 'Flint rings on Farway Hill', *PDAS* 29 (1971) p 167

Radford, C. A. R., The Hurlers, Cornwall, notes on excavations, *PPS* (1935) p134; (1938) p319

Rogers, E. H., Report on the Yelland Stone Row, *PDAES* I (1932) p201. The sites at Westward Ho and Yelland, *ibid* III (1946) p 109

Russell, V. and Pool, P. A. S., 'Excavation of a menhir at Try, Gulval', *CA* 3 (1964) p15, with a list of 17 others examined in Penwith

Simpson, D. D., 'Beaker houses', *Economy and settlement in Neolithic and early Bronze Age Britain* (1971) p138 fig 23 for the Gwithian house

Thom, A., Megalithic astronomy, *Vistas in Astronomy*, edited A. Beer (1965)

Thom, A., *Megalithic sites in Britain* (1967). Both contain plans of some of the south-western stone circles

Thomas, A. C., 'A new cist from Trevedra Common, St Just-in-Penwith', *PWCFC* II (1960–61) p189

Worth, R. H., *Dartmoor* (1953). Stone rows p202; Stone circles p248. For Beakers, see Barrows and Kistvaens p192

Williams, A., 'Bronze Age barrows on Charmy Down, Somerset', *Ant J* XXX (1950) p34

CHAPTER V

Ashbee, P., 'Some Wessex barrow forms in South-west England', *PWCFC* I (1955–6) p132

Ashbee, P., *The Bronze Age round barrow in Britain* (1960)

ApSimon, A. M., 'Cornish Bronze Age Pottery', *PWCFC* II (1957–8)p 36

ApSimon, A. M., 'Dagger graves in the Wessex Bronze Age', *Institute of Archaeology Tenth Annual Report* p 37. Defines the two phases of the Wessex culture

Benton, S., 'The Pelynt Sword-hilt', *PPS* (1952) p 237

Childe, V. G., 'Bronze dagger of Mycenaean type from Pelynt, Cornwall', *PPS* (1951) p95: also Branigan, K., *PPS* (1972) p282

Crawford, O. G. S., 'The ancient settlements at Harlyn Bay', *Ant J* I (1927) p288 for the barrows and *lunulae* at Harlyn

Dudley, D. and Thomas, C., 'An early Bronze Age burial at Rosecliston, Newquay', *CA* 4 (1965) p10

Fox, A., 'The Broad Down (Farway) necropolis and the Wessex culture in Devon', *PDAES* IV (1948) p1

Fox, A., 'The Upton Pyne cemetery', *PDAS* 27 (1969) p75

Fox, A. and Stone, J. F. S., 'A necklace from a barrow at North Molton, Devon', *Ant J* XXXI (1951) p25

Hawkes, C. F. C., 'The double axe in prehistoric Europe', *Annals British School at Athens* XXXVII (1937) p141

Hawkes, C. F. C., and Smith, M., *Inventaria Archaeologia*, Great Britain II (1955) no 9, The Plymstock hoard.

Kendrick, T. D., 'The Hameldon Down Pommel', *Ant J* XVII (1937) p313

Patchett, F. M., 'Cornish Bronze Age pottery', *Arch J* CI (1944) p 29; CVII (1950) p 49. Classes B and C for ribbon-handled urns

Piggott, S., 'The early Bronze Age in Wessex', *PPS* (1938) p 52. The classic article defining the Wessex culture

Piggott, S., 'Bronze double-axes in the British Isles', *PPS* (1953) p224

Pollard, S. H., 'Excavation of round barrow 248B, Upton Pyne', *PDAS* 27 (1969) p49

Radford, C. A. R. and Rogers, E. H., 'The excavations of two barrows at East Putford', *PDAES* III (1947) p156.

Renfrew, C., 'British faience beads reconsidered', *Antiquity* (1970) p199. States the case for local manufacture

Stone, J. F. S. and Thomas, L. C., 'The use and distribution of faience', *PPS* (1956) p37. The case for Mediterranean origin. See also McKerrell, H, *PPS* (1972) p286

Taylor, J., 'Lunulae reconsidered', *PPS* (1970) p38

CHAPTER VI

ApSimon, A. M., and Greenfield, E., 'Excavation of the Bronze Age and Iron Age settlement at Trevisker Round, St Eval', *PPS* (1972) p302

ApSimon, A. M., 'Bronze Age pottery from Ash Hole, Brixham', *PDAS* 26 (1968) p21

Ashbee, P., *The Bronze Age round barrow in Britain* (1960)

Borlase, W. C., Typical specimens of Cornish barrows, *Arch* XLIX (1886) p181

Chanter, J. F., Examination of one of the Chapman barrow group, *TDA* XXXVII (1905) p93

Christie, P. A., 'Crig-a-Minnis: a Bronze Age barrow at Liskey, Perranzabuloe, Cornwall', *PPS* (1960) p76

Fox, A., 'Celtic fields and farms on Dartmoor', *PPS* (1954) p87

Fox, A., 'Excavations on Dean Moor, 1954–6', *TDA* LXXXIX (1957) p18

Fox, A. and Britton, D., 'A continental palstave from the ancient field system on Horridge Common', *PPS* (1969) p220

Godwin, H., 'Prehistoric trackways of the Somerset level', *PPS* (1960) p1

Gray, H. St G., 'Excavations at Combe Beacon, Combe St Nicholas', *P Som AS* LXXXI (1935) p83

Gray, H. St G., 'Double-looped palstave from Curland, Taunton', *Ant J* XVII (1937) p63. See also H. N. Savory, *PPS* (1949) p128

Grinsell, L. V., 'Barrows of North Devon', *PDAS* 28 (1970) p95

Grinsell, L. V., 'Somerset Barrows: I. West and South', *P Som AS* 113 (1970) p1

Hawkes, C. F. C., 'The Towednack gold hoard'. *Man* (1932) no 222 p117

Hawkes, C. F. C. (editor), *Inventaria Archaeologia*. Great Britain I (1955) No 4, The Crediton Hoard

Hodges, H., 'The Bronze Age moulds of the British Isles', *Sibrium* V (1960) p 153

Langmaid, N., 'Norton Fitzwarren', *Current Archaeology* 28 (1971) p116, interim report

Mercer, R., 'The excavation of a Bronze Age hut-circle settlement, Stannon Down, St Breward', *CA* 9 (1970) p17

Miles, H., 'Stenalees barrows, St Austell, interim report', *Cornish News Letter* (1972)

Radford, C. A. R., 'Prehistoric settlements on Dartmoor and the Cornish Moors', *PPS* (1952) p55

Rodgers, E. H., 'The excavation of a barrow on Brownstone farm, Kingswear', *PDAES* III (1947) p164

Thomas, C., 'Tredarvah, Penzance', *CA* 3 (1963) p85

CHAPTER VII

Allen, D. F., 'The Origins of Coinage in Britain', *Problems of the Iron Age* ed S. S. Frere, *Inst of Arch* occ p, No 11 (1961) p 97. Coins found in the south-west are in the gazetteer p 145; hoards p286

Allen, D. F., 'The Paul (Penzance) hoard of imitation Massilia drachms', *Num Chron* 7th ser I (1961), p91

Bulleid, A. H. and Gray, H. St G., *The Glastonbury Lake Village*, i and ii (1911, 1917): *Meare lake village*, i–iii (1948, 1953) p 196. See also Tratman, E. K.

Clarke, P. J., 'Finds from Mount Batten, Plymouth', *PDAS* 29 (1971) p137

Cotton, M. A., 'Cornish cliff-castles', *PWCFC* II (1958–9) p113

Crawford, O. G. S., 'The ancient settlements at Harlyn Bay', *Ant J* I (1927) p283

Crofts, C. B., 'Maen Castle, Sennen', *PWCFC* I (1955) p98

Dudley, D., 'An excavation at Bodrifty, Mulfra, near Penzance', *Arch J* CXIII (1956) p1

Dudley, D. and Jope, E. M., 'An Iron Age cist burial from Trevone, North Cornwall', *CA* 4 (1965) p18

Fox, A., 'Two Greek silver coins from Holne, S Devon', *Ant J* XXX (1950) p152

Fox, A., 'Excavations at Kestor', *TDA* LXXXVI (1954) p39 for iron-working

Fox, A., 'Hill-slope forts and related earthworks in south-west England and South Wales', *Arch J* CIX (1952) p1

Fox, A., 'South-western hill-forts', *Problems of the Iron Age* ed S. S. Frere, *Inst of Arch* occ p, No 11 (1961) p35

Fox, A., 'An Iron Age bowl from Rose Ash, N Devon', *Ant J* XLI (1961) p 186

Fox, A., 'The Holcombe mirror', *Antiquity* (1972) p293

Fox, A., and Pollard, S. H., 'A decorated bronze mirror from an Iron Age settlement at Holcombe, Devon', *Ant J* LIII (1973) p1

Fox, A., Radford, C. A. R. and Shorter, A. H., 'Report on the excavations at Milber Down, 1937–8', *PDAES* IV (1949–50) p27

Fox, Sir C., *Pattern and Purpose* (1958). The mirrors p84

Fox, Sir C., 'Triskeles, palmettes and horse-brooches (the Polden hoard)', *PPS* (1952) p47

Gordon, A. S. R., 'The excavation of Gurnard's Head, a cliff-castle in W Cornwall', *Arch J* XCVII (1940) p96

Hawkes, C. F. C., 'The ABC of the British Iron Age', *Problems of the Iron Age* ed S. S. Frere, *Inst of Arch* occ p, No 11 (1961) p1. Sets out a chronological scheme

Leeds, E. T., 'Excavations at Chun Castle, Penwith', *Arch* 76 (1926–7) p205

Liddell, D. M., 'Excavations at Hembury Fort, Devon', *PDAES* I (1930) p40; (1931) p90; (1932) p162; II (1935) p135

Megaw, V., 'The Trenoweth collar', *CA* 6 (1967) p5

Megaw, V., 'Later Iron Age collars from western Britain', *BM Quarterly* XXXV (1971) p145

Ordnance Survey, *Map of Southern Britain in the Iron Age* (1962)

Peacock, D., 'A contribution to the study of Glastonbury ware from S.W. Britain', *Ant J* XCIX (1969) p41

Peacock, D., 'A petrological study of certain Iron Age pottery from Western England', *PPS* XXXIV (1968) p414

Radford, C. A. R., 'Report on the excavations at Castle Dore', *JRIC* new series I (1951) p1

Richardson, K. M. and Young, A., 'Report on the excavations at Blackbury Castle', *PDAES* V (1954–5) p43

Saunders, A. D., 'Excavations at Castle Gotha, St Austell' Interim report, *PWCFC* II (1960–1) p216

Threipland, L. M., 'An excavation at St Mawgan-in-Pyder', Cornwall, *Arch J* CXIII (1956) p33

Tratman, E. K., 'The Glastonbury lake village; a reconsideration', *P Bristol Univ Spelaeological Soc* 12 (1970) p143. For another approach, see D. Clarke, 'A provisional model of an Iron Age society and its settlement system', *Models in Archaeology* (1972) p801

Whybrow, C., 'Some multivallate hill-forts on Exmoor', *PDA* 25 (1967)

Willis, L. and Rogers, E. H., 'Dainton earthworks', *PDAES* IV (1951) p79

CHAPTER VIII

Andrew, C. K. C., 'Trevelgue Head promontory fort, note, Roman Britain in 1939', *JRS* XXX (1940) p175

Brown, P. D. C., 'A Roman pewter mould from St Just in Penwith', *CA* 9 (1970) p. 107

Clarke, E. M., *Cornish fogous* (1962)

Cunliffe, B., 'The Somerset levels in the Roman period', *Rural Settlement in Roman Britain* ed C. Thomas, *CBA* (1966) p68

Douch, H. L. and Beard, S. W., 'Excavations at Carvossa, Probus', 1968–70, *CA* 9 (1970) p93

Dudley, D., 'Excavations on Nor'Nour', *Arch J* 124 (1967) p1

Fowler, P. J., 'A native homestead of the Roman period at Porth Godrevy, Gwithian', *CA* I (1962) p17

Fox, A., *Roman Exeter* (1952); see also *Arch J* CXIV (1957) Exeter meeting p 178, where references given to later work

Fox, A., 'Excavations at the South Gate, Exeter, 1964–5', *PDAS* 26 (1968) p1

Fox, A., *Exeter in Roman Times* (Exeter 1971). This summary is now out of date in respect of the military occupation, since it was written before the 1971–2 excavations. Interim reports have now been published by J. Collis, *The Guildhall Site* (Exeter 1972), and by M. Griffiths, *The Cathedral Close* (Exeter 1972), but excavations are still in progress and conclusions are not finalised. I am much indebted to Mr Griffiths for information and many friendly discussions of the outstanding problems, but I take the responsibility for the tentative solutions in this chapter, pending the full reports

Fox, A., Roman objects from Cadbury Castle, *TDA* LXXXIV (1952) p105

Fox, A. and Ravenhill, W. D., 'A Roman Signal station on Stoke Hill, Exeter', *TDA* XCI (1959) p71

Fox, A. and Ravenhill, W. D., 'Early Roman outposts on the north Devon coast', *PDAS* 24 (1966) p1

Fox, A. and Ravenhill, W. D., 'The Roman fort at Nanstallon, Cornwall', *Britannia* 3 (1972) p56

Fox, A. and Ravenhill, W. D., 'Excavations at Trevinnick, St Kew', *CA* 8 (1969) p89

Greene, J. P. and K. T., 'Excavations at Clannacombe, Thurlestone', *PDAS* 28 (1970) p130

Guthrie, A., 'Excavation of a settlement at Goldherring, Sancreed', *CA* 8 (1969) p5

Haverfield, F. and Taylor, M. V., 'Romano-British Cornwall', *VCH* ii Part 5 (1924)

Hencken, H. O'N., 'Excavation at Chysauster, 1931', *Arch* 83 (1933) p237

Hirst, F. C., 'Excavations at Porthmeor 1933–5', *JRIC* XXIV (1936) p1

Margary, I. D., *Roman Roads in Britain*, I (1955) p104–117

Masson-Phillips, E., 'Excavations at Lower Well Farm, Stoke Gabriel', *PDAS* 23 (1965) p3

Miles, H., Seaton Down excavations 1968–9; the report will probably appear in *PDAS* for 1973; I am indebted to Mrs Miles for advance information

O'Neil, B. St J., 'The Roman villa at Magor farm, near Camborne, Cornwall', *J Brit Arch Ass* XXXIX (1933) p116

Ordnance Survey, *Map of Roman Britain* (1956)

Peacock, D., 'A Roman British salt-working site at Trebarveth, St Keverne', *CA* 8 (1969) p47

Pollard, S. H., The Holcombe villa excavations 1969–71. The report will appear in *PDAS* for 1974: I am indebted to Mrs Pollard for advance information. See also *Ant J* LII (1973) p1

Richmond, I. A., Crawford, O. G. S. and Williams, I., 'The British section of the Ravenna Cosmography', *Arch* 93 (1949) p1. The south-west p17

St Joseph, K., 'Air Reconnaissance in Britain' (North Tawton fort), *JRS* (1958) p98; see also *TDA* XCI (1959) p174

Taylor, M. V., 'The Sidmouth bronze, legionary standard or tripod', *Ant J* XXIV (1944) p22

Thomas, C., 'The character and origins of Roman Dumnonia', *Rural Settlement in Roman Britain*, CBA (1966) p74

Thomas, C., 'Excavations at Mulfra Vean, 1954', *CA* 2 (1963) p23

Webster, G., 'An excavation at Nunnington Park, Wiveliscombe, Somerset', *P Som AS* CIII (1958) p81

Wedlake, W., *Excavation at Camerton, Somerset* (1958). The pewter industry p82

Woolner, A and D., 'Teignbridge and the Haldon road', *TDA* LXXXVI (1954) p211, and XCI (1959) p 149

CHAPTER IX

Alcock, L., *Arthur's Britain* (1971). Chs 7–8 contain an authoritative up-to-date account of the period.

Doble, G. H., *The Saints of Cornwall*, Pt1 The Land's End district (1960). Pt2 The Lizard district (1962)

Fowler, P. J., Gardner, K. S. and Rahtz, P. A. *Cadbury, Congresbury, Som. 1968*. Extra Mural Dept. Bristol Univ. (1970)

Fowler, P. J. and Rahtz, P., 'Somerset AD 400–700', *Archaeology and the Landscape* (1972)

Fowler, P. J. and Thomas, A. C., 'Arable fields of the pre-Norman period at Gwithian', *Cornish Archaeology* I (1962) p61

Fox, A., 'A Dark Age trading site at Bantham, S Devon', *Ant J* XXXV (1955) p55

Jackson, K., *'Language and History in Early Britain'* (1953) for the general background

Macalister, R. A. S., *Corpus Inscriptionum Insularum Celticarum* I (1945). Cornwall, Devon and Somerset, pp435–78

Nash-Williams, V. E., *The early Christian Monuments of Wales* (1950)

O'Neil, H., 'Excavations of a Celtic hermitage on St Helen's, Scilly', *Arch J* 121 (1964) p40

Ordnance Survey, *Map of Britain in the Dark Ages*, 2nd edition (1966)

Peacock, D. and Thomas, C., 'Class E imported post-Roman pottery', *CA* 6 (1967) p35

Pollard, S., 'Neolithic and Dark Age settlements on High Peak, Sidmouth', *PDAS* 23 (1966) p35

Pollard, S., 'Radio-carbon dating of the settlements on High Peak, Sidmouth', *PDAS* 25 (1967) p41

Radford, C. A. R., 'Tintagel, the Castle and Celtic monastery', *Ant J* XV (1935) p401. *Idem* 'Tintagel in history and legend', *JRIC* XXV (1942) p25

Radford, C. A. R., 'Report on the excavations at Castle Dore', *JRIC* new series I (1951) p60

Radford, C. A. R., 'An early Christian inscription at East Ogwell', *PDAS* 27 (1969) p79

Rahtz, P., 'Sub-Roman cemeteries in Somerset', *Christianity in Britain AD 300–700*, ed Barley, M. and Hanson, R. P. C. (1968) p193

Rahtz, P., 'Cannington hill-fort', *P Som AS* 113 (1969), p56

Rahtz, P., 'Castle Dore, a reappraisal of the post-Roman structures', *CA* 10 (1971), p49

Ravenhill, W. D., 'Cornish Dark Age settlement', *Geography* XL (1955) p237. 'Settlement of Devon in the Dark Ages', *TDA* LXXXVI (1954) p63

Thomas, A. C., 'Cornwall in the Dark Ages', *PWCFC* II (1957–8) p59

Thomas, A. C., *Gwithian. Ten Years' work 1949–58* (1958)

Thomas, A. C., 'Imported pottery in Dark Age western Britain', *Med Arch* III (1959) p89

Thomas, A. C., *The early Christian archaeology of Northern Britain* (1971). This contains much that is relevant to the south-west

Sources of Illustrations

The majority of the photographs were specially taken for this book by Mr W. Hoskin, Exeter University photographer, in Exeter, Taunton and Truro Museums and in the field.

The air-photographs, Plates 9, 12a, 13a, 18b, 19a and 23a are from the Cambridge University collection (curator Dr J. K. St Joseph) Crown copyright. Plate 19b was taken by Cdr C. S. Fox, RN.

Plates 3a, 3b, 6a, 11a, 17b, 18a, 23b are from the collection of Mr Charles Woolf, MPS., of Newquay. Plates 7a, 10a, 10b, 15, 20b, 24a are reproduced by permission of the Trustees of the British Museum. Plate 24b is reproduced by permission of the Ancient Monuments Branch of the Department of the Environment; Plate 11b, Plymouth City Museum; Plates 13b and 13c, Professor Charles Thomas; Plate 14b, the National Museum of Antiquities of Scotland; Plate 22, Exeter City Council.

The co-operation of all these individuals and public bodies is gratefully acknowledged.

For the second edition the following photographs have been added: Plate 1c, by permission of Dr N. Savory; Plates 4a, 4b, 4c, by permission of Dr John Coles; Plate 20a, British Museum; Plate 21b by courtesy of Watts, Blake and Bearne, photograph by Graham Powell.

The maps have been redrawn mostly from my originals by Mr H. A. Shelley, Miss M. R. Bethell and Mr R. Fry. Fig 50 is based on the Ordnance Survey's map of Roman Britain, Fig 55 on Britain in the Dark Ages, both with minor modifications and additions.

The original drawings, many based on work in the field, were drawn by Gillian Lamacraft (Fig 4, 10, 12, 14, 16, 20, 21, 33, 36, 37, 38, 44, 52 and 53), Christine Wilkins (Fig 9, 12, 13 and 26), Gillian Jones (Fig 22 and 35), Rosemary Campbell (Fig 18), and A. Clark (Fig 25). Fig 5 is reproduced by permission of Professor Stuart Piggott; Fig 11, Bernard Wailes; Fig 13, C. A. R. Radford; Fig 16, Paul Ashbee; Fig 38, Mrs P. Christie; Fig 42, Mrs L. Murray-Threipland; Fig 49, R. P. Wright; Fig 53, Mrs E. V. Clark, to all of whom grateful acknowledgement is made.

For the second edition the following have kindly allowed me to reproduce their work: Fig 6 and 39 (redrawn), D. Peacock; Fig 19, V. Russell; Fig 32, N. Langmaid; Fig 56, L. Alcock; Figs 17, 26, 27, 28, 29, 30, 31, 33b, 40, 41, 46, 47, 48 are from my own published works; excepting Fig 17, unpublished. Fig 7 is based on Fig 6, *South-West England*, 1st ed.: additions, *PPS* 1971, Yorkshire; *PPS* 1972, East Anglia and South-West England; and on information from C. N. Moore, Lincolnshire and Nottingham; and Isobel Smith.

Of the new figures, Figs 7, 17 and 48 were drawn by Robert Turner, Figs 6 and 39 by H. A. Shelley, and Figs 46 and 47 by Professor W. Ravenhill and R. Fry. I am indebted to the Editor of *Antiquity* for Fig 6.

Index

(S) indicates that the site is in Somerset; (D), in Devon; (C), in Cornwall.

226